# Hands-On Training

# A Publication in
# the Berrett-Koehler Organizational
# Performance Series

*Richard A. Swanson &*
*Barbara L. Swanson*
*Series Editors*

Other books in this series include

*Analysis for Improving Performance*

*Corporate Creativity*

*Effective Training Strategies*

*Human Resource Development Research Handbook*

*Structured On-the-Job Training*

*Results*

*Training Across Multiple Locations*

# Hands-On Training

## A Simple and

## Effective Method for

## On-the-Job Training

GARY R. SISSON

BK

**Berrett-Koehler Publishers, Inc.**
**San Francisco**

Berrett-Koehler Publishers, Inc.
450 Sansome Street, Suite 1200
San Francisco, CA 94111-3320
Tel: (415) 288-0260 Fax: (415) 362-2515 www.bkconnection.com

ORDERING INFORMATION

Quantity Sales. Special discounts are available on quantity purchases by corporations, associations, and others. For details, contact the "Special Sales Department" at the Berrett-Koehler address above.

Individual Sales. Berrett-Koehler publications are available through most bookstores. They can also be ordered direct from Berrett-Koehler: Tel: (800) 929-2929; Fax: (802) 864-7626; www.bkconnection.com

Orders for college textbook/course adoption use. Please contact Berrett-Koehler: Tel: (800) 929-2929; Fax: (802) 864-7626.

Orders by U.S. trade bookstores and wholesalers. Please contact Publishers Group West, 1700 Fourth Street, Berkeley, CA 94710. Tel: (510) 528-1444; Fax: (510) 528-3444.

Printed in the United States of America

Printed on acid-free and recycled paper that is composed of 85 percent recovered fiber, including 15 percent postconsumer waste.

Library of Congress Cataloging-in-Publication Data
Sisson, Gary R.
  Hands-on training : a simple and effective method for on-the-job training / Gary R. Sisson.
    p. cm.
  ISBN 1-57675-165-1
  1. Employees—Training of. I. Title: Hands-on training
  HF5549.5 T7 S579 2001
    658.3'124—dc21                                    2001025257

Cover and Interior Design: Bookwrights Design
Editorial Services: PeopleSpeak
Indexing: Rachel Rice

First Edition

05 04 03 02      10 9 8 7 6 5 4 3 2

This book is dedicated to the millions of workers who share skills with others in the interest of safety, quality, and productivity. You are the backbone of our economy.

# Contents

# Preface

## Low-Cost, High-Return Training

As a training practitioner, I have spent a good deal of my working life documenting jobs and developing systems to help people learn. For over thirty years I have applied numerous up-to-date training methods and have found it fascinating to watch the evolution toward more and more systematic approaches to learning. Yet as effectiveness and efficiency have increased, so has the cost of developing sophisticated training programs. And unfortunately, training professionals still have little ammunition when they face skeptical managers who often weigh the cost of doing nothing at all against what they view as the high cost and unpredictable results of formal training. For all the changes in my chosen profession, that's one aspect that has changed very little.

When the situation doesn't justify a large expenditure or when the choice is to do nothing, the alternative is not "no learning." The learning will happen anyway. It won't be structured or systematic or efficient, but it will happen because motivated workers will find a way to muddle through, doing the best they can with what they have. And what they have is usually some form of unstructured on-the-job training (OJT): probably the single most expensive training method available. The cost of the resulting inefficiencies will simply be buried beneath the numbers on a chart of accounts as decision makers brag about how much they saved by avoiding a large (and obvious) expenditure to develop formal training. I learned this the hard way, and as I began to sense the inevitability of on-the-job training, I also began to see that the approach had power waiting to be harnessed. So I began to experiment with structures for on-the-job training that could provide inexpensive and reasonably effective training alternatives based on sound learning theory mixed with more than a little common sense. This book summarizes what I have learned. Starting with a research project at Bowling Green State University in Ohio[1] and continuing to this day, the elegant concept of introducing structure into on-the-job training consistently has yielded amazing results in terms of learning, training time, productivity, financial gain, and just about any other type of return available. Hands-On Training is truly low-cost, high-return training.

I wrote *Hands-On Training* primarily for on-the-job training instructors: supervisors and skilled workers who actually train others. I use the book to supplement instructor training seminars for clients where most participants are not professional trainers. They are not theorists. Most are part-time instructors. They include skilled office workers, lab technicians, software engineers, machine operators, truck drivers, customer service representatives, miners, assemblers, nurses, and warehouse workers. They come from high-tech aerospace, computer, and biotech companies as well as old-line industries such as machine shops and food, steel, and automotive companies, to name just a few. While they come from all walks of life, my repeated observation has been that on-the-job training instructors are very serious about their responsibilities and are searching for ways to make their training better. These instructors persevere in the face of many obstacles. Most of them are open and ready to accept help when it is practical and straightforward. When they see Hands-On Training, they know it will work.

If you share this observation or if you're willing to experiment, I say leave the fads and fancy stuff in the training center. Teach workers how to do on-the-job training—and teach them to do it well! Hands-On Training is on-the-job training that works. Use it to help new on-the-job training instructors get started, support your own instructor training, or provide experienced instructors with a fresh perspective. Many on-the-job training instructors will grasp it like a life preserver!

# A Word about Semantics

A new book gets read several times before it is printed for publication. The publisher has editors and reviewers who make suggestions about style and content. And as the author, I had more than a dozen friends read the manuscript and give me their thoughts as well. I got a lot of good suggestions, but one troublesome pattern emerged during this process. Almost every single reader suggested that I change words used to identify some of the most important people and ideas in the book. The first couple of times I changed the words, only to have subsequent readers suggest I change back to those I used in the first place. It was a frustrating experience.

- Is the person who delivers Hands-On Training an instructor, a facilitator, or a teacher?
- Is the person on the receiving end a trainee, a student, or a learner?
- Is the training about skill, expertise, or a subject?

Perhaps you can see my dilemma. I couldn't find words that would satisfy everybody. While all of these words have shades of meaning that may appeal to different types of readers, they are also nearly identical in many ways. So I hope that you will bear with me when I refer to the instructor, the trainee, and the skill. I am doing this only in the interest of simplicity and consistency. Please feel free to substitute your own favorite alternatives. They won't change the message of this book.

Gary R. Sisson
Littleton, Colorado
April 2001

# Traditional On-the-Job Training: Popular but Obsolete

If you are reading this you are probably already an on-the-job train-ing (OJT) instructor or preparing to become one. This being the case, you are participating in one of the most powerful processes on earth—that of passing on your own knowledge and skill to others.

Your challenge may be to train new workers in "the basics," or it may be to train experienced employees in new skills. You may be facing the start-up of a new facility or the launch of a new product or service. You might be assigned to help your organization deal with a changing technology or the implementation of improvements to a job. Your chal-lenge could even be "all of the above."

Regardless of the circumstances, training is an important responsi-bility that sometimes can be as painful as it is rewarding. But the rea-sons for reading this book are to minimize the pain, to gain insight into the process of on-the-job training, and to learn from the experience of others who use training to unleash the power of people. On-the-job training is the single most used (and misused) of all approaches to training. It happens whenever an experienced person shows an inexperienced person how to do a job. Sound familiar? It should because just about everyone who has ever held a job has been exposed to on-the-job training in one form or another.

On-the-job training probably started when one caveman used grunts and gestures to train another caveman on fire starting, spear making, or some other basic skill. You can see it now in a flashback: Ogg sits on a rock, showing Ugoo how to chip away at the flint to make a projectile. Ugoo then tries to make his own spear point while Ogg attempts to help. And there you have it—the dawn of on-the-job training. Today John concentrates on Judy's screen as she demonstrates how to use a database. Then John tries to duplicate Judy's computer skill. A lot has changed. Or has it?

On-the-job training has a long tradition that dates from the Middle Ages, when mothers trained daughters in skills of the hearth, knights trained squires in military skills, and guilds began training apprentices in the various crafts of their day. Through the Industrial Age and into the age of information, jobs and skills have become increasingly complex, but the method of having an inexperienced person learn from an experienced person remains essentially unchanged, even today. The traditional on-the-job training method is characterized by four features:

## 1. Traditional on-the-job training is focused on the work.

The instructor's primary mission is to complete the work at hand. The training is secondary, and little, if any, allowance is made for the presence of a trainee on the job. Thus, if something goes wrong during the training process, the instructor's priority is to get the work back on track. The trainee is expected to stay out of the way, in the interest of productivity. As long as the work gets done, the instructor can do as much training as he or she wants. But make no mistake: the work comes first.

### 2. The work provides the structure for the training.

The training itself is unstructured and relies on the flow of work for its sequence. If tasks occur out of order, so does the training. If a random event happens in the middle of a step-by-step procedure, the instructor interrupts the sequence to deal with it. This being the case, a trainee may participate in some incidents that are highly unusual and altogether miss seeing other, more common events. In a very real sense, the traditional on-the-job training instructor is at the mercy of circumstances. The instructor has only limited control over the training because the work comes first.

### 3. The instructor relies on job experience to do the training.

An on-the-job training instructor usually is a highly skilled employee with years of job experience who is assigned to pass on this experience and skill to a trainee. While the instructor may be an expert at the job, he or she is usually not skilled as a trainer. Some highly skilled workers simply aren't interested in training. Others would like to be trainers but don't know how. Many of us know on-the-job training instructors who are rather poor teachers. That's because most of them have never been trained to instruct.

Compounding this problem is the fact that in most traditional on-the-job training, instructors usually aren't required to teach a standardized method of doing the job. Rather, instructors tend to be left to their own devices when it comes to the specifics of training. Thus, if two instructors have different ways of accomplishing a task, so will their respective trainees. At best, this contradicts the notions of standardization and repeatability, and at worst it could lead to safety or quality problems.

### 4. The training method is determined by the instructor.

In traditional on-the-job training, the instructor chooses his or her own training method. There is no prescribed "best way" to teach a skill. The two most common approaches are showing and telling. Some instructors commonly do a lot more showing than telling or vice versa. Some instructors may provide guidance as the trainees practice, while other instructors may prefer to cover the subject and then put the train-ees to work on the job without much supervision. Needless to say, this may result in spotty performance.

Normally, no formal evaluation is conducted as part of traditional on-the-job training. The criteria for success are determined by the in-structor, and if he or she happens to be methodical, the trainee may become a highly competent performer. But if the instructor is impa-tient, erratic, or under pressure to put the trainee to work, the trainee's skill level may suffer. Either way, the end of training is strictly a judg-ment call on the part of the instructor: the trainee is ready when the instructor says so.

By now it is probably clear that this book does not advocate the traditional approach to on-the-job training. The reasons for this are many, but they all add up to one very fundamental problem: *Tradi-tional on-the-job training is an uncontrolled training situation that can-not produce consistent results.*

In today's world, where concepts such as repeatability, reliability, standardization, and consistency are critical to success, we are mistaken if we use traditional on-the-job training as our training method of choice. Our world (and our customer) demands a better way. Here is why:

- *Traditional on-the-job training is inconsistent.*

    On-the-job training is governed by the individuality of each instructor's approach to training. No standard training method ex-ists and most often there is little, if any, standardization of the job method. This being the case, how can we reasonably expect tradi-tional on-the-job training to yield consistent results in the form of workers who all do the job the same way with the same level of qual-ity? The answer is, we can't. In many organizations dominated by on-the-job training, people with the same job have difficulties even com-municating with each other because they use different terminology for tools, steps, processes, and materials.

- *Traditional on-the-job training is inefficient.*

    In on-the-job training, you have an instructor and a trainee, both working on the same job. Therefore, by definition, on-the-job training is an approach that features two people doing the work of one. If there were a standard level of productivity per worker for the job (such as a numeric quota) the level would be cut in half during the entire training period. It is unlikely that productivity would go up. In fact, productivity may well drop because the trainee might slow down the process. Yet you still have two people on the same job. This fact would suggest that the training should be completed as fast as possible. However, traditional on-the-job training is governed by the work, and the process of learning is disorderly because of continual interruptions in the interest of getting the job done. This tends to slow down the trainee's learning and stretch out the training. Thus, the inherent inefficiency of on-the-job training is multiplied and labor costs increase.

- *Traditional on-the-job training is ineffective.*

  At best, the effectiveness of training accomplished by traditional on-the-job training is open to question because little, if any, attempt is made to evaluate performance during the training period. At the end of training, we seldom really know how much the trainee can do. Only after placement on the job can we tell how well the training worked, and at that point, all too frequently there is no turning back, even with a marginal performer on the job. The demand for productivity is just too great these days.

  An even greater effectiveness problem occurs over the long term. Maybe you experienced it as a child. People sit in a circle. One person whispers a message in the next person's ear. The message gets passed around the circle, and everyone has a good laugh when the heavily distorted message is compared to the original version. The distortion is called "chain loss," and it is exactly what happens to skills as they are passed down from one worker to the next in traditional on-the-job training. A skill may become so diluted and distorted over time that products actually change and we complain about the "lost art" of doing this or that job.

  In fact, on-the-job training's fatal flaws became obvious in the United States during the 1940s, when many American workers left their jobs for World War II and were replaced by new and unskilled workers.

While the times demanded rapid and effective training for a massive new workforce to perform at high levels of productivity and quality, traditional forms of on-the-job training simply couldn't meet these requirements. To deal with the situation, the Training within Industry Service of the War Manpower Commission determined that a standardized training method would be superior to traditional on-the-job training.[2] The group devised a now-famous training system called "Job Instruction Training," which had four steps:

1. *Prepare the learner*

2. *Present instruction*

3. *Try out performance*

4. *Follow up*

Job Instruction Training was highly effective in preparing workers to accomplish wartime jobs. It was used for decades following World War II. However, as time went on, the use of Job Instruction Training diminished, and today, relatively few people even remember its existence. But the Job Instruction Training movement spearheaded a general migration away from traditional on-the-job training toward more systematic, formalized training programs. That movement continues to this day with many types of highly sophisticated training, up to and including interactive systems that are delivered by computers and CD-ROM. These programs are developed and managed by professionals. They are often very effective and efficient ways to train people. At the same time, however, these systems may be complex and very expensive to develop. This may amount to a limitation because the cost of developing training must be spread across those who participate, and in many organizations, the number of trainees is relatively small. So, while more systematic forms of training may work very well, their use is frequently limited to highly standardized work that must be performed by large numbers of workers. On-the-job training, on the other hand, is frequently used in rapidly changing situations, where maybe only a few people need to be trained.

Like it or not, on-the-job training still fills a major role in the over-all scheme of workplace training. And for all its inconsistency, ineffi-ciency, and ineffectiveness, traditional on-the-job training is still the dominant approach. Just as there are reasons for the problems with on-the-job training, there are at least four very compelling reasons for con-tinuing to use on-the-job training as a major training resource.

### 1. On-the-job training is a hands-on approach.

No matter what method is used, from the most systematic pro-gram to the least, training always ends with the trainee doing the real job, whatever it may be. This gives on-the-job training a special appeal to many people—particularly those who learn best by doing. On-the-job training is essentially a hands-on training approach that is an ideal method of supplementing other approaches. Even when formal train-ing programs are used in a training center, they usually end with the trainee undergoing on-the-job training as a follow-up. So in one sense, on-the-job training actually is an inescapable element within almost all job training, especially when a person must continue to learn and re-fine skills that go beyond "the basics." When on-the-job training fol-lows the use of a formal training system, it tends to pick up where the basic training stops. This is a natural and effective application of the on-the-job training approach.

### 2. On-the-job training includes realistic practice.

On-the-job training provides the trainee with opportunities to prac-tice skills under the most realistic conditions possible: actual job con-ditions. Anything less than that requires the trainee to transfer what is learned (in a classroom, for example) from training conditions to job conditions. Many workers have trouble transferring skills from one situ-ation to another. For these people, the more specific the training, the better. Thus, if on-the-job training is able to capture the essence of per-formance in the real world, this is a desirable feature of the approach. In on-the-job training, training conditions and job conditions are the same. Frequently, this makes learning easier and enhances the transfer of training to the job.

### 3. On-the-job training is a simple training approach.

We live in a time of radical changes. The headlines are full of up-heaval all around us every day. But while earthshaking changes rock the business world and radically alter some jobs, other jobs are in a con-tinual state of evolution, with many smaller changes due to improve-ments in work methods, equipment modifications, and the addition or revision of systems. While revolutionary changes may call for the de-velopment and implementation of formal training systems to alter the way work is done on a grand scale, many of the smaller, evolutionary changes don't justify such a high level of effort and investment. At the same time, however, implementation of small, "everyday" changes may frequently require some degree of training. These small changes are prime targets for on-the-job training because on-the-job training is essentially a simple training approach that is easily adapted and ap-plied without the costly developmental efforts usually associated with formal training. While major, earthshaking changes are the ones that get publicity, the vast majority of changes fall into the "everyday" cat-egory. Does that mean they are unimportant? Not at all. Incremental changes may not justify developing a special system, but success could well hinge on the application of a simple system (on-the-job training) to make sure workers understand new ways of doing their jobs.

### 4. On-the-job training is the ideal informal training system.

Training has long been thought of as a management or organiza-tional function. But the reality is that most training is informal and carried out by the workers themselves. It happens like this: One worker walks up to another worker and asks, "Can you show me how to do this job?" As soon as the experienced person agrees to help (in other words, about 99.9 percent of the time), informal on-the-job training is under way. No manager asked them to do it. No company program is required. No diploma is offered. And nobody even thinks twice about doing it. But this very situation demonstrates one of the most compelling rea-sons for establishing on-the-job training as a key component in any organization's effort to train employees. It is the ideal informal training system, and it is just about inevitable that on-the-job training will occur. When properly done, on-the-job training constitutes the integration of learning with the work itself. This is a highly desirable feature of the on-the-job training approach.

## The Bowling Green Study

In 1975, Bowling Green State University in Ohio conducted what has become a landmark study on the effects of on-the-job training. This study is one of the only pieces of carefully controlled research ever done on the subject. In the study (officially named the "Industrial Training Research Project"), two groups of twenty workers were hired and trained to operate a small but realistic manufacturing process.[3]

The first group was trained using a traditional unstructured form of on-the-job training, which researchers called the "buddy system." The first worker was trained by the supervisor, and then each person trained the next one to do the job. The second group of twenty was also trained one at a time. However, in this group, each worker was trained by the supervisor using a very simple but structured program of on-the-job training.

The results were astounding. The second group reached a predetermined level of skill and productivity in about one-quarter the time it took to train workers by the buddy system. In addition, those trained by the structured on-the-job training approach produced 76 percent fewer rejects, and their troubleshooting ability was increased by 130 percent. While no one has ever tried to duplicate the Bowling Green study, a number of published research reports verify different aspects of the results. All in all, the Bowling Green study makes a very credible case for building structure into on-the-job training.

## Chapter Summary

On-the-job training happens whenever an experienced worker shows an inexperienced worker how to do a job. It is probably the most used (and misused) of all training approaches. While several fallacies and "fatal flaws" are associated with the traditional approach to on-the-job training, there are some equally compelling reasons why on-the-job training is needed. Nearly all of the problems associated with traditional on-the-job training may be overcome by introducing structure into the system, and that brings us to the single most important conclusion of this chapter: *If we're going to use on-the-job training anyway, let's use it well.*

The remainder of this book explains how to do just that. It is not magic and it isn't even complex. For the most part, using on-the-job training well is a matter of mixing a little knowledge and a lot of common sense into a simple, practical system. That is exactly what makes it so very powerful.

# Improving Results with Hands-On Training

Tim Horton was having a tough time on his new job. He knew it, his boss knew it, and so did everyone else. It wasn't as if he didn't try, but the computer system was complex, and there were a lot of applications to learn. Tim spent a week in formal training and had done well. Once he got on the job, however, he couldn't keep up with the workload. Two of Tim's coworkers had tried to help, but it didn't work. Tim just wasn't catching on.

Tim's boss, Shauna Davis, was feeling the pressure to replace Tim with someone who could get the job done. But Shauna was reluctant to bring in yet another new person while there was still a chance that Tim might improve. "Maybe it isn't Tim's fault. Maybe he isn't getting the right kind of help. After all, there is a difference between the classroom and the job," she thought.

Shauna decided to have Tim work with Linda Hart, who was one of the very best people in their department. Linda was the semi-official department trainer and had been to a class on how to conduct Hands-On Training. But Linda was very busy. If she was going to help Tim, it would have to happen fast—three or four days at the most. They couldn't afford more than that.

Linda met Tim in the break room. She spent a few minutes getting to know Tim better and asked about his training so far. Then they went out to Tim's area and Linda watched him work for a while. As she watched, Linda began to notice a couple of patterns. Tim was going through too many steps, and he was making a number of mistakes. He was making the job more complicated than it really was. Linda asked if she could show Tim a couple of better techniques. She went through each one step-by-step, clearly explaining what to do. One procedure at a time, she had Tim do the job. As Tim practiced, Linda watched carefully. She asked him to say what he was doing and why. When Tim got it right, she told him so. When he made a mistake, she showed him how to do it better and had him try again. She asked questions to make sure Tim really understood. This went on for the rest of the day. It was smooth, it was natural, and it was effective.

The next morning Linda started by reviewing what they covered the day before. Then she had Tim go back to work while she watched. Linda was very careful to give Tim all the help and advice he needed. After a couple of hours, she started to leave Tim alone for short periods, and by noon, Linda felt confident about leaving Tim to work on his own.

Scenes like this one are repeated every day in countless workplaces where Hands-On Training is used. Maybe it's for a brand new employee. Maybe it's because of a promotion or transfer. Maybe the person has had prior training—maybe not. Maybe the person is having trouble, like Tim, or maybe it's a start-from-scratch situation. It doesn't matter. Hands-On Training is on-the-job training that works. It's smooth, it's natural, and it's effective.

Hands-On Training promotes the integration of on-the-job training into a system or structured approach to training. Job Instruction Training, as described in chapter 1, was an early attempt to add structure, and it was successful but only up to a point. The method advocated in this book is a descendent of Job Instruction Training but modernized for application in today's world.

The Hands-On Training method was developed by Denver-based Paradigm Corporation, a firm that specializes in on-the-job training. Paradigm consultants recognized the inevitability of on-the-job training, as well as its value in training people to do jobs. However, they also recognized that fundamental problems plagued traditional on-the-job training. A more systematic approach was needed. For some time, Paradigm consultants experimented with Job Instruction Training, but eventually they concluded that critical elements of modern-day training were underemphasized, and a better method was required. The method they developed, Hands-On Training, is easy to remember and easy to use. It is a sequence of events that flows naturally from one step to the next. The Hands-On Training method has six steps:

# HANDS-ON TRAINING (HOT):

1. **P** ➤ **Prepare for training.**

2. **O** ➤ **Open the session.**

3. **P** ➤ **Present the subject.**

4. **P** ➤ **Practice the skills.**

5. **E** ➤ **Evaluate performance.**

6. **R** ➤ **Review the subject.**

If you can remember the simple acronym HOT POPPER, you can remember the steps of Hands-On Training. Of course, there is more to using the method than just remembering the steps. But even the list of steps shows how straightforward and natural the Hands-On Training method is.

## Remember When

We asked a number of people to recall their experiences with Hands-On Training. Here are just a few:

### The Bad Old Days

Chonita Ramos, a Hands-On Training instructor from Colorado, remembers the way things used to be. She recalls, "New people never even had a chance to learn their jobs. They were just thrown in and most of them quit after the first couple of days. It was horrible. Nothing ran right. But now that we can train them, it's a better place to work and we're doing much better."

### The Start-Up

Ronnie Moss, a human resources manager from Georgia, reflects about using Hands-On Training to accomplish a very important project. He says, "Not only did we develop and present a training program which led to an extremely successful start-up, but many of us benefitted personally. Together we met one of the greatest challenges our organization will ever have."

### The First Day

G. R., a warehouse worker from Ohio, remembers his first day on the job. "They turned me over to this guy who was supposed to show me the job. He left me standing alone next to a railcar for two hours. I was lost and I had no idea what to do. Finally my supervisor came by. After that they had me work with a *real* trainer for the rest of the day. Once she took over, everything just fell into place. She calmed me down and showed me how. Then she had me practice the job. It really helped me."

Before we get into the details of HOT POPPER, an example may help put the system into perspective. This example demonstrates a very common on-the-job training situation that could happen in almost any work setting: an office, a store, a factory, a mine, a bank, or a hospital. It could happen almost anywhere that an experienced person trains an inexperienced person on how to do a job. Here's the scenario:

### 1. Prepare

The instructor is assigned to train an inexperienced person on the job. To prepare, the instructor reviews notes, thinks about what to say, and decides how best to demonstrate the proper job procedures. The instructor also gets mentally ready to teach and makes sure everything is ready in the work area. This happens before the training begins.

### 2. Open

The trainee arrives, and the two people spend a few minutes talking, getting to know each other better. The instructor then introduces the subject to be learned and explains its importance. Also during this time, the instructor finds out what, if anything, the trainee already knows because this might affect where to begin. In some cases, the opening step might be used to calm down a trainee who is nervous about learning the job. When the instructor is satisfied that the trainee is ready, he or she moves on.

### 3. Present

After placing the trainee in the best position to see and hear, the instructor carefully shows and explains the proper way to do the job. The trainee's job is to pay close attention and ask questions. To make sure the trainee isn't overwhelmed, the instructor is careful to stop before covering too much material. This implies that the instructor must focus attention on the trainee. In many cases, the instructor may repeat the demonstration, and sometimes the trainee may be asked to explain what the instructor is doing. When the instructor thinks that the trainee is ready, he or she asks if the trainee would like to try out the job. If the answer is no, the instructor continues the presentation. When the answer is yes, the instructor moves to the next steps.

### 4 and 5. Practice and Evaluate

Practice and evaluation often happen simultaneously. As the trainee demonstrates how to do the job, the instructor may ask questions or have the trainee explain each step. At the same time, the instructor observes and listens very carefully to make sure the trainee gets it right. As the trainee practices the job, the instructor offers feedback, especially on the parts that are well done. To help the trainee progress, the instructor then has the trainee practice the job again. But before the next trial, the instructor shows, explains, and gives guidance on how the trainee can improve his or her performance. This pattern continues until the instructor is convinced that the trainee can perform the job correctly.

For larger, more complex jobs or skills, the training is usually broken down into smaller chunks and first practiced part-by-part, as described above. Then near the end, the trainee is required to practice the whole job for some period of time, while the instructor evaluates performance.

### 6. Review

To wrap up, the instructor may ask and answer any final questions. Usually the instructor will summarize both the steps of the job and the trainee's performance during practice, expressing confidence that the trainee can do the job. The instructor will then make a work assignment or lead into the next part of training. When the trainee begins working on a job assignment, the instructor will continue coaching and gradually taper off as the trainee comes up to speed on the job.

This type of structured on-the-job training is repeated countless times every day where Hands-On Training is a way of life. It isn't really a training program in the normal sense. Rather, Hands-On Training is a tool that becomes a natural part of the work itself. However, the way the HOT instructor leads the training is critical to its success. When it is given only lip service, HOT is just traditional on-the-job training in disguise. But when it is properly applied, Hands-On Training has three characteristics that make it incrementally more powerful than traditional on-the-job training:

*1. The training follows a step-by-step system.*

*2. The trainee learns the "official" method of doing the job.*

*3. The instructor is trained to use HOT.*

A closer look at the steps of the HOT POPPER method will reveal a number of instructional routines and substeps that contribute to the overall effectiveness of Hands-On Training. Within each of the six main steps is a specific sequence for the HOT instructor to follow.

# Step 1: Prepare for Training

Any experienced instructor will tell you that preparation is probably the single most important element in successful training—that means any kind of training, including on-the-job training. This being said, it is important to define the scope of preparation as it is described in this book.

One meaning of "preparation" includes the analysis and documentation of jobs, up to and including writing a training program. While this is certainly a legitimate (and highly desirable) form of preparation, it is not the subject of this book. A number of other books offer detailed explanations about how to design and write training programs. However, precious few books explain how to use those programs. So we have left the subject of preparing training materials to others and pick up where they stop—at the point where the materials are ready for use by HOT instructors.

As a HOT instructor, you may or may not have a well-documented training program. Even without one, it is possible to do a credible job of Hands-On Training because the system itself forces a degree of standardization, and the method is viable either with or without formal job documentation. So with this in mind, let us consider the following thoughts on preparation for Hands-On Training. Before any HOT session begins, everything must be ready to go. It is the instructor's responsibility to prepare the session for success. The three major areas of preparation are the instructor, the materials, and the training area. All three work together to make HOT successful.

## Assume Responsibility

By definition, an instructor is in a leadership position. This means that you must accept the responsibility that goes along with the job. Training doesn't succeed or fail because of luck. It succeeds or fails because we make it do so. And as the instructor, it is your job to make training succeed. Quite literally, the choice is yours!

Many situations in a person's life can cause stress, uncertainty, and fear. Getting married, moving, starting a new job—all of these events may cause one's anxiety level to go up. Another is being an instructor. The point is that if you get a little tense about the idea of becoming an instructor and having to deal with new people, you're not alone. In fact, if you weren't just a bit nervous, there would probably be something wrong. It is entirely normal to feel tension about training another person. One question to ask about any type of fear or anxiety is, "Is the fear realistic or not?" To answer that question, you first have to ask another one. "What am I afraid of?" In many cases the answer is that you are afraid of failure. You are afraid that you'll forget what to say and embarrass yourself. Now, is that fear realistic or not? The answer depends on how you handle the situation.

As with any goal in life, the degree to which you accomplish the goal of being a good instructor depends on the degree to which you prepare. If you set yourself up for failure, you will self-destruct. If you set yourself up for success, you will probably become a better instructor than you ever thought possible. You are personally responsible for your own success.

## Get Yourself Ready

As an instructor you must be mentally prepared to conduct training. You may or may not have written support materials. If you do, it is critical to study them, including instructor guides, job documentation, and other information about the job, until you can do the training without them. This may mean memorizing, but more importantly it means understanding.

The reason for doing this is important. In most workplaces, handling an instructor guide, thumbing through job documentation, or referring to notes may be very difficult as well as distracting to trainees. These actions make the instructor seem less than competent. Therefore, we strongly recommend that instructors learn both the job itself and the training sequence (from an instructor guide or this book) so that papers may be put aside when the training begins. Our advice is simple: *Leave the written training materials at home. Do the training without them.* This may mean extra preparation time for Hands-On Training, but it's worth the effort.

If you don't have written materials, your preparation problem is somewhat different. It would be a very good idea to spend some time thinking about the job and exactly how you are going to approach the training. In fact, you may even want to create some simple documentation of your own, such as an outline of the main steps. The reason for this is more to help organize your thinking than merely to have something in writing. Whether or not you have documentation, your mental preparation is a very important component of Hands-On Training.

During preparation, try to picture the session in your mind. What will you say? How will you demonstrate the job to be learned? What questions can you anticipate? How will you answer them? What questions will you ask the trainee? What problems can you expect? How will you handle expected problems? By visualizing the session, you will become mentally prepared. Make sure you can do everything you ask the trainee to do. If you can't actually do the job yourself, you'll find it much harder to teach others to do it. The best HOT instructors are experts in the job they're teaching.

## Assemble Training Materials

If certain materials are to be used by the trainee, make sure these are available and ready to be used. Training materials may include software, hardware, samples, various training aids, documentation, booklets, paper-and-pencil exercises, tools and equipment, machinery, raw materials, instruments, forms, drawings and blueprints, parts—anything at all that is used to support the training. Training materials must be available in sufficient quantity, operating properly, and placed near the area where they will be used.

## Set Up the Area

Set up the area so that the trainee can see. Decide on the best position for yourself and the trainee. If someone will assist you during the training, decide where the assistant will work so the trainee's view isn't blocked. It is critical that the trainee is able to see the details of a job demonstration. If the job requires moving from one area to another, decide the best way to do this.

It is best to choose a quiet area for training. If the actual work area is noisy, decide how to handle this problem. You might have to select a second, quieter area and move back and forth. Clean up the area to show the best possible example of good housekeeping. When training is done in a messy area, trainees might assume that the mess is acceptable—even normal. We suggest that this type of impression is both undesirable and lasting.

Double-check all training materials. These should be laid out in an orderly manner, ready for use. If safety equipment is required, make sure it is available and working. If the job is one where workers get dirty, have the proper cleanup materials available. When everything is ready, step back, look over the area, and ask yourself, "Will this area give the trainee the impression I want to give?" If not, go back to work until it does.

It is difficult to overemphasize the value of solid preparation before starting Hands-On Training. A new instructor usually struggles with preparation the first few times. With just a little experience, however, most instructors learn what works best for them and preparation becomes far more efficient. It is interesting to note that the best, most highly experienced HOT instructors are among those most dedicated to preparation. One might think that these people would "have it down pat" and wouldn't need to prepare. On the contrary, most outstanding HOT instructors have learned that good preparation is the single most important factor in their success.

## Step 2: Open the Session

The purpose of this step is to introduce the subject and help the trainee get ready to learn the job. The instructor should accomplish this before starting to present the details of training. Two important goals should be accomplished in the opening step. The first is to help the trainee calm down and get into the proper frame of mind for learning. The second is to establish the "big picture" of the job at hand.

## Put the Trainee at Ease

Many people are tense and nervous as they begin training. They must become more comfortable in order to learn. A nervous trainee will tend to be distracted from the subject at hand and will have extra difficulty learning the job. Therefore, you must do everything possible to put the trainee at ease and make sure he or she is ready. Otherwise, the training will be off to a bad start.

Greet the trainee with an easy, friendly manner. This doesn't require a long, drawn-out conversation. It simply means a short, relaxed introduction to let the trainee know it's okay to relax a little. Some instructors will meet a new trainee in a break area, sit down, and chat for a few minutes over a cup of coffee. Also remember that a smile will go a long way toward getting the process off on the right foot.

No matter how you do it, let the trainee know you're a real human being and there is no reason to worry. Developing a comfort factor is especially important with a trainee you don't already know. If you have worked with the trainee before, a friendly greeting normally will be a good start.

## Explain the Objective

Briefly explain what's going to happen: "The job we're going to cover is (state the job)." This statement should be clear and definite so there is no mistake about the subject.

If your training program includes formal training objectives, this is when to explain them. If not, explain any job requirements, such as productivity or quality goals, or other criteria that are used to define a job well done. Sometimes it may be a good idea to show the trainee the finished product or the end result of the effort. The point here is to let the trainee know what will be expected at the end of training. This may include passing a test of some type, but more often it is merely doing the job in a way that meets certain standards of performance. It is also appropriate to explain how the evaluation of performance will take place.

## Determine the Entry Level

Each trainee comes with his or her own entry level. There would be very little point in training a person to do a job that the person already knows. On the other hand, a trainee might not have the basic skills that are needed to begin training on the job at hand. More often, however, the trainee will have some degree of knowledge or skill but will still need your help. A good instructor will determine the trainee's entry level and tailor the training accordingly.

To determine a trainee's entry level, ask specific questions to find out what, if anything, the trainee already knows about the job to be learned. In so doing, your questions must be very specific and to the point. If you ask generalized questions and accept vague answers, it is possible to be misled. If the trainee claims to know the job, ask more questions to find out exactly how he or she goes about it. Before you make a decision about whether or not to continue training, make sure the trainee uses the work method you want. Have the trainee *show* you how he or she does the job. Remember that sometimes people think they know more than they really do. On the other hand, if your trainee already knows how to do the job, why waste time with more training?

## Provide Reasons to Learn

Most people learn only when they are ready to learn, and if a trainee thinks the training is pointless, he or she may have very little, if any, motivation to learn the job. Yet the job exists for a reason, and usually a rationale exists for doing it a certain way. This being the case, there are also reasons for the trainee to take an interest in the training.

A good way to help motivate the trainee is to establish the importance of doing the job correctly. It isn't necessary to spend a lot of time "selling" a trainee on the job, but the trainee should know the reasons for learning to do the job properly. To provide motivation for learning the job, focus the trainee's attention on issues such as quality, safety, the consequences of doing the job wrong, and the value of doing it right.

# Step 3: Present the Subject

In this step, the instructor demonstrates the operation exactly the way it should be done on the job. If the method is complicated, break it down into smaller "chunks," and train on each part. Only one way of doing the job should be shown during initial training. This method should be the official way of doing the job, without taking shortcuts. This will help avoid confusion and increase the probability of standardization.

The point of training is to make complicated things simple and easy to understand. Using showing or telling alone is not enough to ensure success. An effective presentation uses telling, showing, and illustrating with examples. Show the trainee how to do the job. Explain the method as you go. When it will speed up learning, give the trainee samples or examples of what you mean.

## Position the Trainee

The best demonstrations are those where trainees can see and hear well. This isn't always easy to accomplish, so it is very important to address these issues during preparation. Think about the best location for the training and also think about where to position the trainee. In many cases it is better to have the trainee look over your shoulder than it is to show a mirror image of the job.

Place the trainee in a position where he or she can clearly see your demonstration of the job. Ideally, the trainee should be facing the work, as if he or she were actually doing the job. Also make sure your own hands don't cover up what you are trying to show.

## Start a Two-Way Demonstration

Good demonstrations are engaging they hold the trainee's attention and interest. One way to accomplish this goal is by having a conversation with the trainee throughout the demonstration. Not only does this tend to engage the trainee, but also it ensures that your message is being received and understood. As you begin to show the job, talk to the trainee in a conversational way, setting up a normal two-way communication process.

It is tempting, but not very effective, to demonstrate a job all the way through and then talk about the whole process later. While this might speed up the demonstration and create fewer problems for the instructor, it will probably lengthen the overall training period because without two-way communication, it is nearly impossible to tell if the trainee really understood. Instead, talk over each step while you show how it's done. Encourage your trainee to ask lots of questions during the process. Questions and discussion make people think, and that will speed up the training.

## Go Step-by-Step

Cover each step separately and clearly before moving to the next step. Go slowly, and be very methodical. The demonstration should be very easy for the trainee to follow. This type of orderly presentation speeds up learning. As you cover each step, be sure to explain any words or jargon that a new person might not understand. Remember, what seems simple and obvious to you might be something entirely new to your trainee.

As you show and explain the job, remember that the method you demonstrate will be the one the trainee will follow. It is very important that you show the best technique possible for a new person and explain why the job should be done that way. Sometimes highly skilled workers may take shortcuts that should never be attempted by a new person on the job. Avoid these shortcuts, and concentrate instead on the official version of the job.

In many cases, the official method is written down in some form of job documentation. Most job documentation breaks down a job or task into discrete steps. If you have this type of documentation, it is wise to study it during the preparation step. If no formal documentation is available for the job, make an outline of the steps. There are at least two good reasons for this. First, it will help to clarify your own thinking about the job. This, in turn, will go a long way toward helping you explain the job thoroughly. Second, the outline will improve the probability that you will cover the job method the same way each time you present the training. Remember, consistency is a central issue when it comes to on-the-job training.

## Stress Key Points

Don't just mention important details, *stress them!* Usually only a few details make a job difficult or tricky. But if a trainee misses them, he or she might fail on the job.

Key points can be stressed in several ways. One is repetition: the instructor goes over important points at least twice. Another is to visually exaggerate certain steps or movements that are important. A third way to stress points is to provide support in the form of a training aid, written material, samples, or anything else that will tend to remind the trainee of the point. A fourth way is to include the key points in question-and-answer sessions during the training.

## Be Patient

Some trainees may take a while to catch on. Showing impatience with such trainees only creates more tension and stress, which tends to slow down learning. The instructor's job is to keep the trainees in the right frame of mind. Many trainees are supersensitive to even the slightest signs of impatience or annoyance from the instructor. So in the interest of learning, always remain very patient, steady, and calm.

## Avoid Information Overload

In a new job, trainees commonly suffer from "information overload." This means that too much information comes at them too fast and they start to get confused. The instructor must be sensitive and back off when this happens. Sometimes this means slowing the training. Sometimes it means going over points again until you're sure the trainee understands. The three biggest traps for instructors are (1) going too fast, (2) overcomplicating, and (3) not sticking to the subject. In each of these cases, the trainee will tend to get confused, and learning will suffer.

You can tell when a trainee has reached the point of overload by being observant. When the point of overload is reached, people tend to turn off and shut down. Their eyes might seem to glaze over, they usually become restless, and their attention starts to wander. These are signals that it might be time to slow down or take a break. Certainly it is time to create more involvement, perhaps by asking questions.

## Demonstrate Twice

The best instructors demonstrate at least twice. Repeating a demonstration tends to "lock in" the training. Usually the second run-through is faster and very worthwhile. Because the trainee has already seen the job once, the second demonstration may be a good time to encourage more questions and dialogue. Some instructors have the trainee give a verbal explanation of what's happening as the instructor performs each step. This technique provides a smooth transition from the presentation step to the practice step.

## Set Up the Practice

At the end of your second demonstration, ask if the trainee is ready to try the job. If not, demonstrate again until he or she feels ready to practice.

Be aware that a trainee might be somewhat intimidated and therefore reluctant to try a new skill. As the instructor, on the other hand, you may sense that the trainee is ready for practice and may think that further demonstrations won't improve the trainee's ability to perform. In this case, you should encourage the trainee to give the job a try. Assure the trainee that you are there to help and will assist as needed. The point is to gently nudge the trainee closer and closer toward doing the job.

One key ingredient in setting up a practice session is to explain how the practice will work. Make the assignment crystal clear. Explain exactly what the trainee is supposed to do. Also explain what you will do as the instructor. That way, there will be no surprises. It may sound simple, but a practice session is often less effective than it should be due to confusion on the part of a trainee.

# Step 4: Practice the Skills

In Hands-On Training, the practice step is where the trainee performs the job while the instructor observes and provides feedback on performance. The practice and evaluation steps usually happen simultaneously. This is because skill is developed through practice by trying out performance under realistic conditions. And the best time to evaluate performance you can see is during a practice session.

In a practice session, the role of the trainee is to do the job. The role of the instructor is to evaluate and provide *positive* coaching to guide the trainee toward success. In a very real sense, this is where the instructor shapes the trainee's performance, almost like modeling clay. The idea is to have the trainee practice the skill, get feedback and coaching, repeat the practice, and try to improve until the instructor is satisfied with performance.

One practice session may cover only part of a total job. This is especially true when the job is complex, requiring many different skills or procedures. If this is the case, it is best to practice parts of the job in separate sessions. Then it is appropriate to have a final solo evaluation (see step 5, below) to make sure the trainee can perform the entire job.

## Let the Trainee Try

Have the trainee do the job while you watch and evaluate. The first time through, it isn't important to have the trainee explain what he or she is doing. But if the trainee seems ready, ask him or her to explain the operation during the demonstration. Provide helpful hints as needed.

## Make Practice Realistic

Sometimes instructors get nervous when it comes time for the trainee to actually put his or her hands on the equipment. What if the trainee makes a mistake? What happens if the trainee flips the wrong switch? Does the whole department shut down? It can be risky, but sooner or later the trainee is going to have to actually do the job (the sooner the better in most cases). That is why most practice should be done under realistic working conditions. Whenever possible you should have the trainee do exactly what he or she will be required to do every day.

Yes, sometimes it is possible that a trainee's mistake might really shut down the whole department. That's when to simulate—but only those very risky steps. Have the trainee just pretend to do those, and then require a detailed explanation of exactly when, how, and why each risky step is performed. When you are satisfied that the trainee knows what to do, move on to the real job. And be ready to step in yourself, if needed.

# A Pattern for Effective Practice

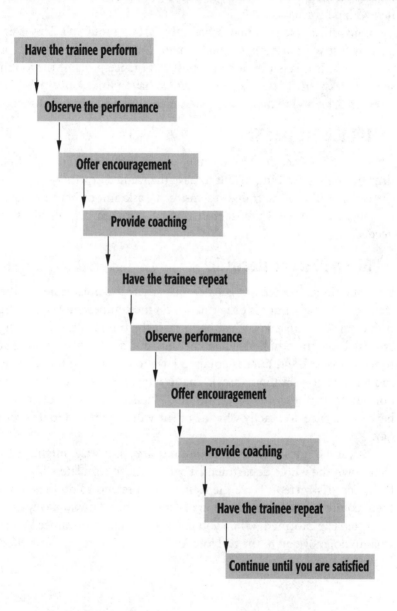

Have the trainee perform

Observe the performance

Offer encouragement

Provide coaching

Have the trainee repeat

Observe performance

Offer encouragement

Provide coaching

Have the trainee repeat

Continue until you are satisfied

# Step 5: Evaluate Performance

It is important to remember that the practice and evaluation steps of HOT POPPER are intertwined. They almost always happen together. The best way to develop a skill is to have the trainee practice while you provide coaching and then repeat that pattern until you are satisfied with the performance. For that reason, we will continue our discussion of practice as it is combined with evaluation.

## Observe Carefully

You must watch the trainee carefully to make sure the job is being done properly. Make sure you are in the right position to see any important movements. Remember that some movements (keystrokes or mouse clicks, for instance) happen very quickly and that others are subtle. During practice, ask yourself the following questions:

- Is it being done correctly?
- Is it being done in sequence?
- Is it being done safely?

If you are going to help a trainee improve performance, it is critical that you provide that person with very specific, helpful suggestions. By observing performance carefully, you will be able to pinpoint exactly what went right and what went wrong. This in turn will provide the type of specific information you need in order to guide the trainee toward successful job performance.

## Offer Encouragement

While the trainee practices, offer praise for correct performance by making statements like "Yes, that's good," "That's right," or "Good . . . you seem to be getting it," or "Nice job," or even "Uh-huh." These simple expressions reinforce the good performance and keep the trainee headed in the right direction. They are essentially forms of encouragement that provide guidance for performance.

If you decide to summarize the practice session, start with what went right. If you have carefully observed the trainee's performance, it should be relatively easy to offer specific praise for parts of the job done well.

## Provide Coaching

While simple forms of encouragement such as those listed above tend to be quite effective, the effects of criticism are far less predictable. Statements of criticism such as "Wrong!" "You just made a mistake," "Uh-uh," or "Nope" frequently become barriers to good performance. We would advise instructors to eliminate offering criticism altogether and replace it with helpful coaching.

Even though you don't want the trainee to develop bad habits, it is usually more effective to refrain from coaching until just before the person is ready to begin another practice session. This doesn't mean that you should ignore errors—rather, it is a matter of timing and how you handle them. The best time to coach a trainee by offering tips or other help is *not* after the practice is over but rather just *before* the person tries again. So if you see the trainee do something wrong, it automatically means that you should have the person practice at least one more time. Sometimes this means stopping practice in the middle, providing some extra instruction, and starting over.

When this happens, it is important to understand that stopping practice in the middle, providing help, and starting again follows the rule. The help is provided immediately *before* resuming the practice session.

One exception to this "rule" is that any unsafe acts on the part of a trainee must be stopped immediately to avoid a possible accident.

## Make Coaching Helpful

Coaching is helpful only if it tells the person exactly what and how to change. If your coaching is vague or the trainee doesn't understand exactly what to do, it will be very difficult to improve performance. This implies that coaching must be offered in the form of specific suggestions for improvement.

In training, the point isn't to emphasize what a trainee did wrong. The point is to help the trainee do it right. Avoid saying "Now I want to cover a few things you did wrong." Instead, present your suggestions in the form of help. This can be done by saying "Now that you're ready to try again, let me offer a suggestion," or "I want to give you a couple of tips that will make the job easier," or "If you would do such and such, you'll do it even better this time."

## Repeat Performance

Always have the trainee perform the operation at least twice. This makes the training almost foolproof. During the second run-through, insist that the trainee explain what he or she is doing. This explanation gives you one more chance to locate and correct misunderstandings. Then decide if a third run-through is needed.

## Ask Questions

During the second (or third) time through the operation, ask questions to test the trainee's knowledge. The best kinds of questions are those such as the following:

- "Why do you . . .?"
- "How do you . . .?"
- "What would happen if . . .?"
- "What else would you do?"
- "What would you do next?"

## Accelerate Experience

In most jobs, only a small percentage of the work is difficult—the rest is easy to learn. Sometimes you can isolate the difficult parts of the job and have the trainee work on them separately through repetitive drills. Then the difficult parts can be integrated back into the context of the whole job and practiced as part of the overall job sequence.

The effect of doing this is to accelerate the trainee's experience by increasing the number of times the trainee gets to try the difficult skills. For example, the trainee may get to practice the difficult part ten times, while practicing the overall job only twice. This may be more valuable (and much faster) than trying to practice the whole job ten times.

## Stress Method and Quality, Then Speed

The principle here is simple: First do it correctly; then do it fast. In the early stages of practice, the instructor should refrain from pressuring the trainee to develop speed. Instead, the instructor should concentrate on the trainee's ability to follow the correct procedures, make good decisions, avoid common errors, and generally do the job the way it should be done. Then and only then should the instructor encourage the trainee to speed up his or her performance.

## Continue Till You're Satisfied

There is no hard-and-fast rule about how many times to have a trainee practice a skill. The best guideline is to stop when you are personally satisfied that the trainee can do the job or has accomplished the training objectives. When you are confident that the trainee can perform the job alone, move on to either a solo evaluation or the review step of HOT.

## Conduct a Solo Evaluation

Before a new pilot is certified, he or she must take off and fly the plane alone while a flight instructor evaluates. This is the new pilot's "final exam." In Hands-On Training we have that option as well. Usually a solo is done to prove that the trainee can accomplish an objective such as doing the job correctly for a given period of time, producing a prescribed quantity and a specified level of quality. The trainee does the work and the instructor or perhaps someone else evaluates performance. Records are kept. At the end of the solo, the trainee may be officially qualified or certified to do the job. In many cases this is a very good way of bringing closure to the training. It is a logical last step in the evaluation process, which sets up the conditions for the review step of HOT.

# Step 6: Review the Subject

The review step of HOT POPPER is intended to provide a summary and a transition between training and normal, everyday work. At the end of the formal review of training, the trainee is given an assignment, either for work or more training. Assuming that the review is followed by a work assignment, we have included the informal coaching and tapering-off process that usually concludes Hands-On Training.

In the HOT POPPER method, the opening step is meant to cover the big picture of the job. The presentation, practice, and evaluation steps usually break down the job into smaller parts, making it easier to learn. Finally, the review step returns to the big picture by combining the smaller parts into a summary of the entire job.

## Review Performance

Begin by reviewing the trainee's overall performance in the practice session. Cover both strengths and areas where the trainee needs to improve. This is best accomplished by having the trainee first addressing three self-critique questions: What went right? What went wrong? What did you learn? When the trainee is finished answering, it is your turn to summarize performance. It should be relatively easy to be positive at this point. If not, maybe your trainee should still be practicing!

## Review the Instructions

This is an especially good time to keep the message short. Review the main points of instruction. Ask the trainee if there is anything that will get in the way of being able to do the job as required. Answer any final questions that remain.

## Make an Assignment

The instructor should give the trainee an assignment that requires use of the new skills. This allows the trainee to get the feel of the job, while continuing to practice. It is important at this time to leave the trainee alone for a while. The instructor should intentionally go away and let the trainee perform on his or her own. It symbolizes your confidence in the trainee's ability.

## Offer Help

Tell the trainee where you can be located if any problems occur. Usually it is best to insist that the trainee contact *you,* as opposed to another employee. Other employees might have their own ways of doing the job and may create confusion about how the job should be done.

## Release the Trainee

This is the end of formal Hands-On Training, but you still have a responsibility to follow up and help the trainee reach top performance.

## Follow up Frequently

During the early stages of follow-up, it is best to check in with the trainee to make sure everything is okay. This gives you a chance to provide more coaching and answer remaining questions. How often you check will depend on how well the trainee is doing on the job.

## Encourage Questions

Usually, most of the trainee's questions will have been answered during the actual Hands-On Training. But sometimes a nagging question keeps bothering a trainee. Encourage the trainee to ask any final questions. Of course, it is also entirely possible that the trainee may encounter a situation that wasn't covered before. This may give rise to additional questions.

## Taper Off

As the former trainee continues his or her normal job performance, check in less frequently until there is no longer a reason to continue coaching. At this point, the Hands-On Training is complete. There is no set formula or procedure for tapering off coaching. It is very much a judgment call on the part of the instructor.

The one pitfall in following up is the possibility of creating a dependency on the part of the former trainee. Former trainees have a natural tendency to keep in contact with those they respect—such as their instructors. But when this gets in the way of work, yours or theirs, it is an unhealthy situation. Avoiding the dependency pitfall is relatively simple: become increasingly demanding as time goes on.

# Outline: Hands-On Training

### Step 1: Prepare for Training

• Assume responsibility
• Get yourself ready
• Assemble training materials
• Set up the area

### Step 2: Open the Session

• Put the trainee at ease
• Explain the objective
• Determine the entry level
• Provide reasons to learn

### Step 3: Present the Subject

• Position the trainee
• Start a two-way demonstration
• Go step-by-step
• Stress key points
• Be patient
• Avoid information overload
• Demonstrate twice
• Set up the Practice

### Step 4: Practice the Skills

• Let the trainee try
• Make practice realistic

### Step 5: Evaluate Performance

• Observe carefully
• Offer encouragement
• Provide coaching
• Make coaching helpful
• Repeat performance
• Ask questions
• Accelerate experience
• Stress method and quality, then speed
• Continue till you're satisfied
• Conduct a solo evaluation

### Step 6: Review the Subject

• Review performance
• Review the instructions
• Make an assignment
• Offer help
• Release the trainee
• Follow up frequently
• Encourage questions
• Taper off

# Characteristics of Hands-On Training

## Hands-On Training Is a Simple Method

As with any method, Hands-On Training has both strengths and limitations. One of its great strengths is its simplicity. HOT does not require extensive documentation, long development times, or (in most cases) special training facilities. This makes HOT desirable in low-budget situations where an organization lacks funds to, or sees no reason to, develop a more formalized training system. It is truly low-cost, high-return training.

## Hands-On Training Is Instructor Based

The success of Hands-On Training depends upon the skill of the instructor. At the very least, a trained instructor is required. If HOT is attempted by an instructor who isn't trained to use it, some portion of the benefit will be lost. This being the case, organizations that use HOT must also provide a means to train enough instructors for the anticipated number of trainees. While we will say more about this later, it is important to note that limiting the number of instructors may create a problem of elitism that flies in the face of the fundamental value of HOT. If the availability of instructors is a problem, alternative training methods should be considered.

## Hands-On Training Is Flexible

Once you learn to conduct HOT, you can apply it to virtually any job or skill you know. HOT POPPER is a universal training method that needs little, if any, modification to fit different jobs. While specific areas of emphasis may change from one job to the next, the overall method remains the same. The instructor has flexibility within the context of HOT.

## Hands-On Training Is Work Oriented

Hands-On Training is effective when training people in applied skills, such as manual or sensory skills, procedure following, and problem solving. It is best used to teach the types of performance that can be seen. HOT is not a particularly effective system for teaching theory or abstract concepts. Thus, while most job requirements can be learned through Hands-On Training, the underlying theories should be addressed through alternative training methods.

## Hands-On Training Is Best for Individuals or Small Groups

Experience has shown that HOT is a good way to train up to three people at a time. It is not a particularly effective way to train larger groups. The HOT POPPER method requires trainees to engage in one-on-one interaction and practice with a trained instructor. When this is attempted in large groups, trainees have trouble hearing and seeing demonstrations. They also may get bored while waiting for a turn to practice. As individual attention is decreased in Hands-On Training, so is the rate of learning. Thus, if training in large groups is required, it would be advisable to consider alternative methods.

# Chapter Summary

Hands-On Training provides a structure, while maintaining the basic simplicity that gives on-the-job training much of its natural appeal. This provides numerous advantages over the traditional approach to on-the-job training. Hands-On Training turns traditional on-the-job training into a systematic approach for training individuals or small groups of people in job skills. A trained instructor follows six steps to help the trainee learn the job:

## Hands-On Training (HOT):

1. **P** ➤ **Prepare for training.**
2. **O** ➤ **Open the session.**
3. **P** ➤ **Present the subject.**
4. **P** ➤ **Practice the skills.**
5. **E** ➤ **Evaluate performance.**
6. **R** ➤ **Review the subject.**

The acronym HOT POPPER helps instructors remember these steps. In addition, within each of the steps are techniques that allow the instructor to apply the method to a wide variety of skills and jobs.

# Adapting the Method
# to Fit Your Situation

Don't kid yourself. Hands-On Training may follow a formula, but it's not a rigid system. Each time the method is applied, it is being used by people. Their personalities, their situations, and their personal preferences shape just about everything that happens. There are choices to be made, pitfalls to avoid, and opportunities for creativity throughout the process. Perhaps a story may help to illustrate this point.

Recently I was invited to assist a company in the southeastern United States. It was a heavy industrial factory that produced steel wire. Those not familiar with wire manufacturing might find it helpful to know something about the process. Wire manufacturing (called "wire drawing") is part science and part art. To form the wire, a coil of steel rod as thick as your thumb is pulled and stretched (i.e., *drawn*) through a series of smaller and smaller holes (called "dies") by powerful motor-driven pulleys (called "capstans") until it is drawn down to the correct size. The process is fast, hot, noisy, dirty, and relatively dangerous. You can burn yourself, break an arm, get a cut. Accidents can happen in an instant. Wire drawing is hard work, but it is also work that takes a good deal of thought. A considerable amount of technical troubleshooting is required, so job experience is a valuable commodity within the wire industry.

Wire drawing is also a traditional industry. The industry itself has a long tradition that includes the use of on-the-job training for most of the technical training provided to employees. In this case, I was asked to support a joint union-management effort for continuous improvement in the plant. The union-management team had correctly determined that the organization's technical training needed to be upgraded, and it selected my firm to help. We documented jobs and set up a training program that included Hands-On Training. Next we trained a number of HOT instructors. Finally, as is our practice, we remained on-site to coach and help the new instructors get started. That's where I met Wally Norden, a skilled machine operator and the subject of this story.

Wally was a doer: he was always in action. He was the person usually called upon to bail out another operator having trouble on one of the machines. You'd hear his name over the PA (public address) system: "Wally, can you see what's up on the number twelve machine?" "Wally, I need your help on the number seven spooler." "Wally, can you come to the office for a short meeting?" Wally this and Wally that. He was always busy.

Wally also was a really nice guy. Everybody liked him. He was a natural choice to be a HOT instructor because of his personality and his troubleshooting ability. He made quite an impression in the instructor training program by doing a really fine demonstration about the method for determining die sizes required for different wire diameters (a relatively complicated subject). It was clear that not only did Wally know his job, but also he had learned the HOT method well. When I was assigned as his coach, I thought to myself, "This is going to be a piece of cake." As it turned out, I was in for a few surprises.

# The Preliminaries

## Prepare

Wally was assigned to train a young man named Jeff Tyson. Jeff had been working in the warehouse for about a year, so Wally already knew him. Jeff was up for a promotion to operator in the Wire Drawing Department. Wally would be Jeff's primary instructor throughout the training period.

As a first step, Wally read through the existing training materials. While these were nothing fancy, they did give him a clear idea of the progression of training from start to finish. Also, the materials included a number of suggestions about physical preparation of the workplace, tools required, product samples, and reports that would help during the training. At the end of the day, Wally spent a couple of hours getting ready for the training session.

Before the training started, Wally asked if he and I could have a short chat about the training. He wanted to know if I thought he should go through the whole "getting to know you" routine with a trainee he already knew. I acknowledged that there wasn't much sense in doing that, but on the other hand, Jeff would probably be nervous so it might help to have a cup of coffee together before getting started. Also I suggested that Wally find out how much Jeff had already learned just by being at the factory for a year. Wally thought that made sense.

# Training: Day 1

## Open

Wally, Jeff, and I met in the break room to get the session under way. I explained that my job was just to stand back and watch how the training was going but not to interrupt. I suggested that Wally and Jeff just forget about me and do the training. They agreed.

--- **Reflections** ---

The presence of a coach always makes trainees nervous. It helps me (and will help you too) to explain the role so that those actually performing the task aren't constantly looking over their shoulders. Once you've laid out the ground rules, it's time to keep out of the way and let the training take its natural course. The time to provide suggestions is during a break or just before the trainee practices the job again.

---

Jeff said that he'd never had time to learn much about wire drawing, so Wally decided to start with the fundamentals. He explained that the basic training would last about three weeks and then a work and evaluation period would follow during which Jeff would operate the process under guidance. After that there could be a second round of training to review and go into more depth. I planned to spend the first two days working with Wally. The first day they would cover the equipment parts and purposes, and the second day they would begin to cover the job itself.

Wally was nervous at the beginning, but he followed the HOT process well. The training area was properly arranged and everything seemed ready to go. Wally started by covering several important points about safety in the Wire Drawing Department.

Then Wally took Jeff on a short tour of the work area, briefly explaining each of the major components. Immediately, they encountered a problem: the area was so loud that Jeff couldn't hear. At first Wally continued his explanation, but when he realized that Jeff was totally lost, he turned to me and gave a shrug: "What do I do now, Coach?" I suggested two possibilities: stand really close together or move away from the machinery for the explanations. Wally chose the first of these and they continued. When the tour was over, Wally took Jeff back to the break room for an introduction to the product specifications and quality, using samples to illustrate the main points.

## Present: Equipment Parts and Purposes

After the overview, Wally and Jeff went over the equipment again but in a lot more detail. This was specified as a major step in the training program and it was to last for most of the first day. As Wally explained the equipment I began to sense that Jeff was getting increasingly confused. I wondered why. It was difficult to hear, so I decided to move closer. Wally was talking quite fast. He was excited about the subject and trying to link everything together so Jeff could really understand the relationships and how the various systems worked together to produce the product. At the same time, Wally was explaining a lot of "how to" information about the job. I suggested that it was time for a break.

## Reflections

A couple of things are going on here that are common problems in on-the-job training. First, Wally is an expert on this job and he wants to share his knowledge with Jeff. After all, that's the reason for the training. But in his desire to offer a complete and accurate explanation, Wally finds himself buried under levels of complexity far beyond Jeff's ability to understand. Wally needs to slow down and simplify, explaining one step at a time, until Jeff has a solid understanding of the basics. Second, Wally is confusing the issue by mixing explanations about tools and equipment with explanations about the steps of work. Again, this tends to overcomplicate the situation and confuse trainees. Whether the subject is a computer system or a wire drawing machine, first cover the parts of the equipment, tools, software, and so on. Then cover the steps of each task.

During our break, I commended Wally for overcoming the noise problems and following the training plan. Then I made two suggestions. First, I reminded Wally that this program was at least three weeks long. Jeff would learn the process faster if the information came in smaller chunks. There would be plenty of time to connect everything together. Second, I recommended that when covering the equipment parts and purposes, Wally should stick to that subject and refrain from discussing the steps of work until later. The point was to remember that Jeff was a new trainee and it's easy to get into an information overload situation. Wally agreed and asked if it was okay to repeat some of the training in order to make it more clear to Jeff. I thought that was a great idea. Once Wally slowed down, his explanations became much more professional and Jeff really began to learn.

## Practice and Evaluate

It was obvious that Wally was gaining confidence, and he did an excellent job during the practice session. Wally asked Jeff to locate and explain most of the equipment they had covered during the day. As Jeff went through the drill, Wally avoided criticism, asked questions, offered encouragement, and made suggestions. Most of Jeff's answers were correct, but he also was confused about some of the equipment. When Wally sensed a problem, he would let Jeff finish, offer help in the form of a suggestion or clarification, and then have Jeff go over the same piece of equipment again. This is the essence of coaching. By the end of the day, Jeff was able to explain most of the equipment parts and purposes.

## Review

Just before releasing Jeff for the day, Wally reviewed the session and answered a couple of questions that Jeff still had about the equipment. We all agreed to meet at machine number two first thing in the morning. At the end of day one, it was mission accomplished.

# Training: Day 2

On the second day, the focus of training shifted from the equipment to the work. Wally's training plan called for spending the day operating the equipment under normal conditions. Jeff would learn to package the product, perform several quality checks, weld wire ends together, start new coils of steel rod, and add lubricants to the die boxes—all routine tasks in wire drawing.

---

*Prepare – Open – Present – Practice – Evaluate – Review*
For most jobs that contain several tasks or procedures, it is best to complete a "present-practice-evaluate" cycle for each one before practicing the whole job. Breaking down the job into smaller chunks makes it easier to learn.

---

Wally followed the steps of Hands-On Training for each task. He explained the task, demonstrated the steps of work, and then had Jeff practice while Wally watched and evaluated. Then Wally provided some tips on how to improve and had Jeff repeat the practice. The session was going like clockwork until they were about midway into the third task. Suddenly over the PA came a call: "Wally, I need your help on number six—it's an emergency!" Wally was off like a shot. I turned around and he was gone. Jeff and I just stood there looking at each other for about fifteen minutes, and then Wally returned at a fast walk. "Sorry 'bout that. Norma didn't know what to do so she called me. Anyway, let's get back to the training." We did.

We did, that is, for about twenty minutes. Then we heard "Wally, we have a really bad snarl on number seven. Can you get over here, please?" And again, Wally was gone.

## Reflections

Wally's strength is also his weakness. Like many really good HOT instructors, he is a technical expert and the primary person everyone relies on to fix problems. For such instructors, it's a great temptation to drop the training and concentrate on the next troubleshooting problem, but the trainee suffers when that happens. As much as Wally wants to return to his own "comfort zone" (technical troubleshooting), he must force himself to focus on the training for the duration. The best way to do this is to explain to everyone that you're on a special assignment until the training ends. That way everyone will know in advance not to interrupt you.

---

This time when Wally returned, I suggested another break in order to give him some ideas about how to get back on track. First I explained that if he didn't deal with the PA situation right away, they might as well forget about the training—Jeff would never understand the job. Wally could deal with this in a couple of ways. He could have the supervisor tell other operators to stop calling, or he could tell them himself. Wally liked the second approach better, so I "held the fort" while he made the rounds. After that, the day passed rather smoothly and I felt that Wally was a success.

As I look back on those two days, I guess it was wrong to expect that everything would be perfect just because Wally did so well in the instructor training. The fact is, almost every new instructor encounters some kind of obstacle. Maybe it's a self-imposed obstacle or maybe it's inherent to the situation, but Hands-On Training is just like any other job. It's one thing to know the steps of the method and another to apply them in the real world. You have to practice in order to be successful.

# Tools to Enhance Hands-On Training

Several tools or techniques are commonly used by instructors within the context of Hands-On Training. Some of these govern the instructor's basic approach to HOT and may not be obvious to trainees. Others are more procedural in nature and help the instructor carry out certain tasks during the training. As with the HOT POPPER method itself, most of the tools explained here are simple and straightforward. They don't require a lot of complicated reasoning. Most people can readily understand them and use them to increase the effectiveness of training.

The more difficult question is *when* to use these tools, not *how* to use them. In a few cases the answer is obvious. For example, one of the tools (Daily Routine) describes a simple pattern to follow if your training lasts several days. When do you use it? Every day. But others, such as Question-and-Answer sessions and Self-Critiques must be initiated by the instructor on the spot—when called for by the situation. This means that the instructor must have these tools available (i.e., know them), recognize when it is time to pull one out of the tool kit, and then apply it to the situation at hand. Master instructors do this instinctively. New instructors usually have to think about it.

# Show and Tell

This section contains several tips and procedures intended to help make demonstrations more effective. There are obvious advantages to showing the trainee how to properly accomplish a job while offering a thorough explanation of each step. This is an essential ingredient in the HOT POPPER method. However, most demonstrations are done in the workplace and most work areas contain distractions. This implies that the demonstrations so central to the Hands-On Training method may also present difficulties for the instructor. The following tips may help instructors deal with some of the more common situations.

One challenge is to set up demonstrations so the trainee can see everything clearly. Positioning is always an issue. This challenge is compounded when there is more than one trainee. Aside from avoiding the mirror-image problem, it is important to get each trainee close enough to see the details of the demonstration.

During the demonstrations you should move slowly and distinctly when showing physical skills and other actions that may be difficult to see or follow. For example, trainees often encounter difficulty when trying to follow demonstrations that involve computer screens, keyboards, and mice. If the instructor isn't very slow and deliberate, the trainee will be lost immediately and the demonstration will lead to confusion, not learning. In many cases, it is wise to perform one small step, ask if the trainee saw it clearly, then perform the next step, and use that pattern throughout the demonstration. It may be slow, but at least the trainee will be able to follow the steps.

If a group of trainees is watching, it may be necessary to have those in front kneel down so those behind can see. Also, it may be a good idea to rotate people toward the front so everyone has a chance to see. If the group is too large to effectively view the demonstration, smaller subgroups may be required. This is exactly the reason we do not advocate using HOT with groups larger than three trainees at one time.

A second challenge is making sure the trainee can hear you. In some places of work, the noise is almost overwhelming. Our first piece of advice is to choose the quietest area you can find.

Next, avoid shouting. Shouting will only help you lose your voice. Instead, try to stay close to the trainee and project your voice. Speak slowly and distinctly.

Also realize that it may become necessary to move back and forth between the quiet area and the noisy workplace. Most demonstrations require the instructor to point out certain features in the physical environment. These may include the locations of controls, where to get supplies and materials, parts of a machine, locations on a form or computer terminal, characteristics of a product, and countless other visual features. Whether this is done in the quiet area or the workplace, the best way to do this is to turn and point toward the subject, then turn your attention back to the trainee and talk about it. Avoid facing the work during your demonstration. Instead, face the trainee.

Some demonstrations include examples or samples that can actually be handled by the trainee. These may be powerful training aids, but they may also be distractions. The best way to use samples or examples is to give them to the trainee with the appropriate explanation and allow the trainee time to handle them. Then wait till the trainee is finished before collecting them and moving on. The distraction happens when an instructor moves on while the trainee is still focused on a sample, as opposed to the instructor.

# Questions and Answers

The skill of asking and answering questions is certainly one of the most important skills an instructor can use. Questions are one of the best ways to give and get feedback. They create involvement in the training through a dialogue between the instructor and the trainee. Questions may be used to accomplish many objectives in a training session, such as

- Review material
- Check understanding
- Start a discussion
- Get opinions
- Draw out personal experience

The best questions are those that require trainees to think. Questions that start with "Why?" or "How?" or "What do you think about?" are usually the best. Those that can be answered with a simple yes or no are usually the weakest. Questions are usually most effective when they are asked in "chains." In other words, the answer to one question is followed up with another question. In general, a series of connected questions is better than a "one question, one answer" parroting routine. Usually the follow-up questions go deeper into the previous answer. They expand it, test it, or (in the case of a group situation) give other people a chance to express their opinions. This is the essence of dialogue.

Most of the time an instructor has an answer in mind when he or she asks a question. On the other hand, most questions have more than one good answer. A good instructor is willing to accept an answer that may be different from the one he or she expected—especially if the other answer makes sense. If you insist that only your own answers are right, you will be regarded as a rigid instructor.

If a trainee doesn't know the answer to a question, it is your responsibility to help the trainee. Instructors aren't perfect! Sometimes you might ask a question that nobody understands but you. The best policy is to automatically assume that you asked a bad question. Rephrase the question and ask again. Then, if your trainee can't answer, ask yourself what's wrong. Sometimes even the best instructors must answer their own questions.

Try to avoid tricky questions that trap people. These tend to embarrass others, and they usually don't help people learn the subject. In fact, trick questions usually end up making the instructor—not the trainee—look foolish.

It is normal for the instructor to know more about the subject than the trainee. Otherwise, why do the training? But some questions are impossible for the trainee to answer. They are beyond the trainee's knowledge. The rule of thumb is that hard questions make people think, but impossible questions just make them discouraged.

When you ask questions, listen to the tone of your voice. The nature of a question can depend on how it sounds to others. For example, you could ask the question, "Where were you at eight o'clock?" If you used a "normal" tone of voice, the person you asked would probably give you a direct answer. But you could easily ask this question in a tone of voice that sounds like you're accusing the other person of being in the wrong place. Your emotions are expressed in the way your voice sounds. This would tend to put the other person on the defensive and would negatively affect your communication. It is best to ask questions without letting emotion show in your voice.

The kind of questions you ask, the words you use, and the tone of your voice all affect the answers you are likely to get. As an instructor, you will soon begin to realize that questions are a powerful tool. But you also will begin to see that questions are easily misunderstood by trainees. That's one of the frustrations that go with two-way communication.

As with any other skill, the more you practice, the better you become at asking questions. We recommend that instructors ask lots of questions. Questions keep trainees involved, they make people think, and they generally contribute to better training.

# Coaching

Coaching is the process of guiding others to help them reach their full potential. It is a process of shaping or steering performance toward desirable goals. It is possible to have training without coaching and coaching without training. In HOT POPPER, however, training and coaching are used together to help the trainee achieve job performance objectives.

Many people have an image of coaching derived from sports: a crusty old-line coach stands on the sidelines screaming at his players. We believe that this image is both widespread and unfortunate. It portrays what *should* be a very positive process in very negative terms. In Hands-On Training, coaching is entirely positive and intended only to help a person improve. Harsh criticism and any form of yelling at trainees are highly inappropriate. They detract from the learning rather than helping accomplish the objectives.

In HOT, coaching usually happens during the practice step and again during the instructor's follow-up, after the formal training ends. When done effectively, coaching follows a five-step pattern that you can remember by recalling the word *coach*.

## 1. C ➤ Continue Practice

The instructor has the trainee perform a task.

## 2. O ➤ Observe and Evaluate

As the trainee performs, the instructor observes carefully and evaluates performance, noting what the trainee does right and also what needs improvement. The instructor does not interrupt unless the trainee performs an unsafe act or makes a very serious mistake. During the performance, the instructor offers encouragement when the trainee does a step correctly.

## 3. A ➤ Affirm Positive Performance

When the trainee is finished, the instructor compliments the trainee on what went right and then assigns the trainee to repeat the performance.

## 4. C ➤ Communicate Ideas for Improvement

Just before the trainee is ready to perform again, the instructor offers advice, suggestions, or tips on how to improve. These are based on observations of the preceding performance, and they must be very specific in order to be helpful. The instructor also may choose to show the trainee how to improve, rather than merely explaining this.

## 5. H ➤ Help Until Satisfied

The trainee then repeats the performance, trying out the instructor's advice. Meanwhile, the instructor continues to observe, evaluate, and offer encouragement. The instructor might choose to have the trainee repeat only certain steps of the job in order to accelerate experience. If so, the trainee's final performance should cover the entire job or task.

This coaching pattern is repeated until the instructor is satisfied that the trainee can perform as expected.

The HOT coaching technique is intended to be a positive process. For that reason, criticism, in the normal sense, is avoided. Mistakes are dealt with by offering help on how to improve and certainly without dwelling on them. By keeping your coaching positive, you will find that trainees make fewer mistakes and learn faster. Coaching is one more factor that increases the power of HOT POPPER.

# Self-Critique

While coaching is directed and controlled by the instructor, a parallel improvement technique is primarily under the trainee's control. This technique, called a self-critique, can be a useful tool that helps a trainee put his or her performance into perspective. The fundamental principle behind the self-critique technique is that a mistake has only one value: what can be learned from it. As the instructor, your job is to ask the trainee three simple questions: "What went right?" "What went wrong?" "What did you learn?" Then, as the trainee answers, you can offer encouragement as well as advice.

A self-critique allows the trainee to review and evaluate his or her own performance. It also is a means of allowing the trainee to save face by pointing out his or her own errors. In fact, the normal tendency is for trainees to be overly critical of their own performance. As the instructor, your job is to steer the critique toward positive results. Do not allow the trainee to gloss over the first question ("What went right?") or dwell on the negative aspects of performance. Instead, use the self-critique as a means of wrapping up a practice session. Then provide your own coaching and have the trainee repeat the practice until you are satisfied.

# Daily Routine

Hands-On Training is often spread out over several days, sometimes even weeks or months. The same instructor and trainee work together as a team until the trainee can do an entire complex job. In these cases, it is more than likely that the training will be interspersed with work, rather than having one long string of continuous training sessions. There are good reasons for this. One is that a certain amount of work output may be required from both the instructor and the trainee.

Another is that practice tends to be more effective when it is spread out, rather than massed together. On the other hand, the instructor's responsibility is to constantly guide the trainee forward, toward self-sufficiency on the job.

A daily routine will help maintain the necessary balance and enhance progress toward the goal. This simple routine has three elements that can be arranged in any order to fit the situation. You can remember the parts of the routine by recalling these three words: *New, Review, Do*. Here's how it works:

- Every day, spend time helping your trainee learn something new. The goal is to make at least some progress every single day.
- Spend part of the day reviewing subjects covered before. This may entail having the trainee repeat practice sessions from earlier days, it may require you to repeat earlier demonstrations, or it may involve the two of you sitting down and going over some of the material covered in earlier sessions.
- Another part of the day should be spent doing some productive work. This will become easier as the trainee learns more and is able to perform more tasks.

The order of these three segments and their lengths may vary from day to day. The value of this daily routine is that it provides variety while encouraging progress toward the goal.

# Four-Phase Sequence

The Four-Phase Sequence provides a framework or context that helps the trainee see how everything fits together within the job. The sequence is an overall guideline that helps you decide when to cover different subjects. Appropriate steps of the HOT POPPER method are then used to deliver training within each of the four phases. Here is how it works:

- ***Phase 1: Job Overview***
  Explain what the job is. Show the trainee the work area. Cover subjects such as the outputs or products of work, safety and quality issues, performance expectations, objectives, and how the training will work.

- *Phase 2: Equipment Familiarization*

    Cover information about the tools and equipment used on the job. These may include actual hardware and machinery. But they also may include software, forms, reference materials, and anything else that is used to help accomplish the work. The point here is to acquaint the trainee with the language of the job, where materials are located, and generally how they work before getting into the details of actually doing the job.

- *Phase 3: Task Training*

    Use HOT POPPER to cover each job procedure. If the job entails complex setup procedures, cover the normal operating procedures first, then return to the more complicated setup tasks. This way, the trainee will find the setup tasks easier to learn. Save troubleshooting tasks for later in this phase of training. Again, the reason is that it is usually easier for a trainee to deal with exceptions after he or she already knows how to do the job under normal operating conditions.

- *Phase 4: Solo Performance*

    Once the trainee has successfully practiced each task by itself, put the process back together by having the trainee do the entire job under the most realistic conditions possible. The length of this phase depends upon the complexity of the job. The more complex, the longer the solo. The solo phase is often used for job qualification or certification. In addition, it allows the trainee to build confidence and prepare for the transition from training to work.

Chapter 6 of this book contains a set of four instructor guides for Hands-On Training. There is one guide for each of the four phases: job overview, equipment familiarization, task training, and solo performance. Each instructor guide contains specific steps for the instructor to follow during each phase. The HOT POPPER method is integrated into the guides, as are most of the techniques described in this book. The instructor guides are yours to copy and adapt to your own situation.

# Chapter Summary

A number of "tools of the trade" are used by Hands-On Training instructors. Some of these govern the application of Hands-On Training, and others are available for use as needed. All of the following tools are consistent with the HOT POPPER technique:

- Show and Tell
- Questions and Answers
- Coaching
- Self-Critique
- Daily Routine
- Four-Phase Sequence

# Evolution, Revolution, and Execution: Opportunities for Hands-On Training

It's easy to pay lip service to a concept like Hands-On Training. After all, training has been going on since the dawn of humankind. In addition, HOT does not involve complicated theories—it's not rocket science. If you've read this far you already know the concept. You can already "talk the talk." In fact, it is entirely possible that you can talk about Hands-On Training like an expert. The question is, "How are you going to use it?"

Every HOT instructor must answer this question in his or her own way, but maybe a little nudge might help. Let us begin by thinking about the opportunities to use Hands-On Training. Actually, three very common situations may call for the application of HOT: evolution, revolution, and execution.

- Evolution is the situation where Hands-On Training can be used to cover the everyday incremental changes that make an organization tick. This could mean that the system changed over time or we just found a better way of working, as in a continuous improvement situation. Hands-On Training is a great way to "spread the word."

- Revolution is where Hands-On Training may be used to teach people from scratch. This refers to the revolutionary change from "can't do" to "can do." It may involve a brand new employee, an entirely new product or process, or an experienced person on a new job. In many cases, Hands-On Training is the only training option available.

- Execution refers to the use of Hands-On Training to facilitate the transfer of training from the classroom to the job. Hands-On Training is used as a follow-up to other types of training in order to help the trainee make the transition from practicing to properly executing the job in the workplace.

If you think in terms of these three situations, you'll see that the opportunities for using Hands-On Training are countless. They surround you every day. All you have to do is choose. Some of the opportunities are obvious and important while others are more subtle, but every application of Hands-On Training is a "reach out and touch someone" situation. Instructors who decide to apply the principles in this book quickly discover that Hands-On Training is more than just an effective method. It is also a process by which people's lives can be changed for the better. What looks like a cold, step-by-step procedure in the book is warm and flexible human interaction in the world.

The human side of Hands-On Training became evident during hundreds of projects that involved the author and various associates. We share a few of our stories in this chapter with the hope that you'll find some ideas that you can use. As with all interactions involving more than one person, we found different points of view about what happened, depending upon whom we asked. In the case of Hands-On Training, there are almost always three or four sides to the story: those of the instructor who delivered the training, the trainee who received it, the manager in charge of the workplace, and sometimes the training professional in charge of the training program. To get these different viewpoints, we conducted some interviews. At the end of each story, some of those involved will present their thoughts in their own words. It may be enlightening to see what each reveals about his or her role, motivation, and problems. As usual, the names have been changed to protect the innocent.

# Evolution: Software the Hard Way

People who work with computer software will tell you that it's an ever-changing world. It doesn't matter whether you're involved with software development or applications, things are constantly changing. What better place, then, to demonstrate how Hands-On Training may be used to help with evolutionary change?

This example happened in an organization that provides computerized accounting services to smaller retail stores. It also involved the organization's software supplier. A lot of people were affected, but for the sake of simplicity, we will focus attention on just a few of the key players, including Martha Goldberg (the department manager), Sandra McKnight (an internal training professional), and Jerry Kolwiki (a software engineer from the vendor).

The business works like this: Retail stores collect information from their sales receipts and send it to the service company, which then uses a purchased program called MacroMight to calculate the numbers and print reports. MacroMight is provided by the software vendor, and it is constantly being improved and updated. New versions come out monthly, and they would usually result in chaos at the service company.

In fact, that was the reason for Sandra McKnight's job. She conducted classes to teach new employees to use the software but also to update experienced people on new features and procedures. But she found it impossible to keep up with all changes. It was driving her (and everybody else) crazy.

Needless to say, the relationship between the service company and the software vendor was less than cozy. Anybody who passed by the closed-door meetings in the conference room knew that no soundproofing made could prevent the arguments from being heard in the hall. At one point, several people saw Martha Goldberg storm out of the conference room followed by a sweaty Jerry Kolwiki, who was pleading for her to reconsider. The situation was getting ugly. Clearly, something had to give.

Jerry invited Sandra out to lunch. The purpose was to explore how software changes were being implemented and see if there might be a better way. At lunch, both agreed that Sandra was spread too thin. One person simply could not keep everybody updated. After all, over 100 employees were using the MacroMight system. As Sandra and Jerry talked, the topic became how to spread out the training. The obvious answer was to have more people conduct classes, but the company would never agree to that—it would be too expensive. Finally, Jerry suggested the idea of having some of the better employees use on-the-job training to spread the word. Sandra said she might agree to that, but only if the instructors were trained; otherwise, it would be a waste of time. They explored how to train instructors and selected Hands-On Training as the best way. They then trained one instructor from each area—a total of about twenty. The vendor also provided a support system, through which a software engineer and Sandra together briefed the HOT instructors each time changes were made to MacroMight. The instructors then used Hands-On Training to make sure everyone could follow the new procedures.

Was this solution perfect? Not really. There were still some glitches, but the time between making a MacroMight change and getting it online was shortened. The conference room sound level began to drop as the new cooperative training effort took effect. Everybody agreed it was a step in the right direction.

We had seldom, if ever, seen Hands-On Training used in such a hostile situation, so we wanted to find out how it worked. We decided to start by asking the training professional, Sandra McKnight:

> Looking back on it, I wonder how I ever survived those early days. The company decided to use the MacroMight system and we had to make it work. But I was getting so discouraged that I couldn't even sleep at night. When Jerry Kolwiki asked me to lunch, I was just about ready to quit . . . and I'm not kidding.
>
> At first I thought the idea of using on-the-job training was a mistake. I just couldn't see how a bunch of employees were going to deliver effective software training out on the office floor. It's just not a normal kind of training situation. I mean, here you had a group of about twenty new instructors who weren't really trainers and you're depending on them to solve a really major problem. But what I failed

to realize was the effectiveness of the HOT instructor training. I was really surprised. Once they learned the HOT system, our people were just great. And we found out that if we could give them clear, step-by-step software procedures, our instructors could get the word out much, much faster than I could. Quite frankly, it was a great relief.

Next we spoke with Martha Goldberg, the manager:

> I'm not mentioning any names, but I was just about ready to kill somebody over this deal.
>
> We had a tough time, but I think the training worked. I'm reasonably satisfied that we shortened the learning curve, and I know it made Sandra's life easier. So those things alone were worth the cost. But I think there were some other interesting outcomes, as well. For instance, I, for one, was impressed by the way our people responded to the need. I think our instructors really took this seriously and did a wonderful job in their own training. But beyond that I saw people grow. Some of them seemed to rise above themselves and get better in a number of ways I never expected. I really think it was due to being an instructor.
>
> And I'll tell you another thing that impressed me. I didn't get to see the instructor training, but I noticed that the instructors were trying very hard to do their own training in plain English, not a bunch of computer jargon. That impressed me, so I asked a couple of people about it. They said it was part of their instructor training!

Then we met with Tommy Nakamura, who was one of the instructors:

> I was really excited when Martha asked me to instruct. I felt like it was an honor. I know some of the others felt that way too, and we really worked at it. In the first place, the instructor training class was a challenge for me. I had never done this before and I wasn't sure how it would go. But I must admit, I really got into it. Once I got over being so nervous, it was a lot of fun, and I think I'm speaking for our whole group.
>
> But what's really the most rewarding to me is knowing that I'm helping my fellow employees out on the office floor. If you could have seen the problems we used to have, you'd know what I mean. There were people actually in tears out there. We couldn't get the system to work. These people want to do things right. They don't screw up on purpose. If you show them and help them, they'll make it work.

Now, when changes come down, the instructors have a meeting and then we take the new procedures out to the floor. I usually try to show two, maybe three, people at a time. Then I have each one follow the procedure, so I know they can do it. Usually the first one makes the most mistakes and I have to help that person more, but by the third one, they've got it. That's the way I was trained to instruct.

Finally, we talked to several of the workers who were updated by instructors using HOT. Just one comment by Matthew Antinori said it all:

> You wanted to know about the training? Well, to me it didn't even seem like training. I mean training is where you go to class, like before, when things were really screwed up. This was no big deal. Just show me what to do, make sure I can do it, and let me get back to work. To me, the new way is a lot less hassle and a whole lot faster than training. That's what I think.

This was an extreme case, but the fact remains: changes happen all the time. Some are so big that formal training is needed. But many changes can be handled simpler and faster by using Hands-On Training. It's a good way to help an organization evolve.

# Revolution: The Church Ladies

This case is about a recently started factory in the Midwest and how it used Hands-On Training. It is about two instructors with a lot of initiative (Susan Lorenzo and Lucy Flores), their manager (Buddy O'Neal), and a number of trainees.

The factory had been moved to the Midwest from another location. The work done was a complicated process with a lot of different products, many kinds of machinery, and numerous hand operations. Most of the production was done in small orders, so employees had to know several different jobs in order to keep the operation going. During the factory start-up, a team of experienced instructors from another plant had trained all the new employees in the basic skills needed to make the products. But less than a month after the instructors left, employee turnover started and new products were introduced into the factory. With new employees and new skill requirements, production started to slip, and it became clear to Buddy O'Neal that one-time training wasn't enough.

Buddy knew something about training. He had been one of the instructors for the start-up, but now he had absolutely no discretionary time available. Running the new operation was a round-the-clock challenge. At the same time, however, Buddy recognized that on-the-job training was best for his operation and that Hands-On Training was the best way to do on-the-job training. The problem was how to begin.

Buddy decided to bring in an outside expert to train in-house HOT instructors. He arranged for a three-day instructor training program and called for volunteers. About ten factory employees came forward, Lucy and Susan among them. Lu and Sue had been friends since high school. Both were self-described "Church Ladies." Both were moms and both were determined to make the best of their new jobs. They both came through the instructor training with a sense of empowerment that neither one ever had before. They personally decided to make HOT work in the plant. And, as Lu and Sue told us, when a Church Lady decides to do something, she gets it done!

The roadblocks started appearing immediately. No time was available for the training. Half of the new jobs weren't documented at all. A lot of the original training materials were missing. The list went on and on, and the task was beginning to look impossible. But just when matters were looking really dim, the light came on. Lu and Sue said, "Let's keep it simple. Let's just go out and start doing it. We'll get caught up on work, leave our jobs for a little while, and be instructors. Maybe we can even show some of the others how to instruct. That could spread out the work and make things easier."

And with no resources beyond their own determination, Sue and Lu got the job done. They started very small. Every time they trained someone, they kept a record of it. Over the first several weeks they trained maybe twenty people and the impact started to grow. Buddy began to notice that productivity was starting to level out a bit. But what really surprised him was that for some reason, people who were never trained in HOT *seemed* to be imitating Susan and Lucy. Something very interesting was beginning to take shape.

Actually, other employees *were* imitating Sue and Lu as instructors. Apparently, the others realized that HOT was making the situation better and they could see it work. In the end, this factory held more instructor training courses, and eventually about 40 percent of the employees were qualified as Hands-On Training instructors. The training was so spread out that it was going on virtually all the time, just as a normal part of the job.

We were so impressed by what Susan and Lucy accomplished that we just had to learn more about how this happened. We started by talking with Buddy O'Neal. Here's what he had to say:

> When I decided to train instructors, I had no idea where it would go. To tell you the truth, I was sort of disappointed with the people who volunteered. In one way I was correct: out of the original ten, eight of them sort of disappeared into the woodwork after instructor training. But in another sense, I was dead wrong: Susan and Lucy are just amazing. They got this training started and at first I didn't even know it was happening. I thought it had died. But somehow those two managed to keep up with a full workload plus do enough training to start making an impact. Now it's more planned than before. Sue and Lu both spend about 25 percent of their time doing training jobs. Now, of course, they have some administrative support that we didn't have before, but from what I can see, a relatively small dedication of personnel to training is giving me a decent payback.

Next we spoke with the Church Ladies together:

*Susan:* When Buddy asked for volunteers to instruct, I thought, why not? But then, I didn't know what I was getting into. Then in the instructor training I got really worried because I didn't think I could do it, but at the end I felt really great. I mean, here I am, just a high school graduate, and I can be a trainer. I could hardly believe it. Neither could my kids.

*Lucy:* That's for me too. I felt so great when I actually knew I could do the training, but then the reality set in. Remember that part, Sue? It was like everybody just turned their backs on us—Buddy was nowhere to be seen. It was like, "Sorry, but just get back to work. Forget about the training." I started to wonder why we even bothered.

*Sue:* Yeah, that's right. But we forgot what they taught us: Keep It Simple, Stupid! If you make it too complicated, the training will never get done.

*Lu:* And not only that, but just pick someplace and start. Put away all the notes and stuff and just go out and do the training. I think that's what made it work. Of course the method works too, but to me it's just getting started.

*Sue:* Anyway, now they see the results. I always knew the training would work if they just gave us a chance. Now they know it too.

And finally, from a couple of trainees came these thoughts:

*Ned Turley:* Lucy reminds me of my mom. She just takes you under her wing and there's no way you can fail.

*Noreen Smallwood:* When I first got hired, things were really messed up. Then these two women just sort of took over the training. I'll never forget one afternoon when I was trying to bend this piece of metal on a fixture. Susan came up behind me and just watched for a few minutes. Then she smiled that smile of hers and asked if she could show me a different way. All of a sudden I saw the trick. I was one step closer to getting my job right. I know it sounds crazy, but simple things like that make a difference.

*Ben Heddens:* I've worked with both Susan and Lucy, and now I've also worked with some of the other trainers. What makes this place special is that they really care about you. It goes beyond just doing a good job—they really do care. When the time comes, I hope I can get to be an instructor too.

Is this pie in the sky? You decide. These are the facts: Two determined women took HOT seriously and it made a lasting difference in their organization. They had no rank and they had very little support—at first, that is. But by the time they were done, the Church Ladies had quite a bit of informal clout and some real backing from management. Why? The answer is simple: They found a way to use HOT and get results. That's revolutionary.

# Execution: Megan's Transfer

Our final story involves just two people who are both managers. The reason for presenting this case is to show how Hands-On Training may be used to develop skills that fall outside the normal definition of skills as discrete tasks. We are suggesting that structured on-the-job training may be a very effective means of developing some of the "soft skills," such as those used in communication, human relations, and management.

Megan Andrews had recently been appointed to a first-level management position, and she attended a highly regarded management training program to begin developing leadership skills. She did very well in the course, but sometimes it's one thing to perform well in the classroom and quite another to perform well on the job. And unfortunately, Megan rapidly developed a reputation for being unreasonable, intolerant, and just one step short of being mean. While she knew the theories and techniques of leadership, Megan was having a great deal of difficulty applying what she had learned in training to her job as a manager.

About six months after she returned from the training program, Megan's boss had her transferred to another group. This was a conscious decision made to place Megan with a manager named Jerome Davis, who was highly respected for his ability to develop others. Jerome was a savvy trainer, familiar with many techniques, including Hands-On Training and its components of demonstration, practice, and coaching.

Before Megan arrived, Jerome was well briefed about what to expect. But Jerome was not one to blindly accept the judgment of others. Rather, he took his time, observing Megan at work and carefully refining his own assessment of her performance. Jerome decided that if he was going to help Megan, he would have to be very clear and precise. Finally, the day arrived when Jerome was ready to begin. By this time he had a list of specifics that he wanted to work on, one at a time.

In the privacy of his office, Jerome began by asking Megan how her job was going. At first, she put up quite a front, but soon her frustrations began to show. Sensing that the time was right, Jerome began asking more pointed questions and suggesting that there might be alternatives to Megan's current way of handling matters. And finally, when Megan began to acknowledge her problems, Jerome offered to help.

Proceeding one step at a time, Jerome and Megan began working together. He would begin by carefully explaining the skill to be learned. Then Jerome would find a way to demonstrate, sometimes through role-playing. And finally they would practice going through either real or hypothetical situations till Megan seemed to understand good alternative techniques. But then came the task of providing coaching and feedback during Megan's solo performance. The problem was that Jerome was almost never around to see Megan in action on her own. Here's what he did: He assigned Megan to practice the skill in a real-world situation and then come back and tell him about it. When she did this, Jerome would have Megan do a self-critique, and then he would provide positive coaching.

It worked. And the amazing part is that once Megan began to understand how to apply her classroom knowledge, Jerome could throw away the rest of his list. Within less than six months, Megan was back on track. Her transition was complete.

We actually heard about this case by accident, about a year after it happened. We asked both Megan and Jerome for their permission to explore what happened and they agreed. We began with Megan's point of view:

> When I first took this job, I was less than a year out of college. I know I'm intelligent, and I guess I was more than a little arrogant about it. I did very well in my formal management training. But for some reason, by the time I met Jerome I was getting into some bad habits. Fortunately for me, Jerome was willing to help. I really respect two things about that man: his clarity and his patience.
>
> To tell you the truth, it's hard for a person to see what she's really doing. It's like looking into one of those fun-house mirrors where everything's distorted. Jerome was able to help me clarify the specific problems that were holding me back. At first this was difficult for me. For one thing, I didn't completely trust Jerome, and for another, I was sort of "resisting arrest." But once I saw what Jerome was really telling me, the whole picture suddenly became clear. I don't mean to oversimplify, but really there were just a couple of things I did that rubbed everybody the wrong way. Of course, they were a couple of things I did all the time, so I had to struggle to change. But that was okay. I came through it. I'm a better person now. I'm certainly a better manager.

When we spoke with Jerome, we were impressed by his awareness, understanding, and ability to apply the HOT process. Here's what he told us:

> It's really pretty simple. I was asked to help Megan improve her performance. I accepted and she was assigned to my group. I decided to identify the specific problems she was having and I made a list. Then I began a series of private sessions that were a combination of counseling, training, and coaching. These went on for about six months. We would meet about once every other week to review how Megan was doing and take the next step. It wasn't long before Megan started to see the effectiveness of some alternative approaches. She's a sharp lady.
>
> I'll try to explain it in terms of Hands-On Training. As I recall, the first step of the process is to get prepared. This was really critical for me because I knew that there was no way I could help Megan until I understood for myself exactly what was wrong. Sure, I had seen some records and talked with a few people, but that's only part of the picture. So the first thing I did when she arrived in my group was to just leave her alone for a while and watch what happened. I don't remember exactly, but I think I identified maybe five or six specific skills that needed work. Then I needed to make a plan. I decided to work on one thing at a time and I decided to do it myself. I came up with a pattern that's right out of Hands-On Training: show and tell, practice, and coach. But behind it all, the time I spent getting ready was critical.
>
> Then it's open the training session, right? Let me tell you, that first meeting with Megan was tough. Let's just say she was somewhat less than receptive. They say you don't learn anything till you're ready to learn. Well, I had to really work hard to help Megan get ready. But I must say, once Megan started to realize that I wanted to help her, not punish her, she started to open up. I think that was the real starting point. From that time on, we really started to work together.
>
> From then on it was pretty straightforward. I would try to explain the skill and show her the alternatives. Sometimes I would demonstrate the skill myself. Sometimes we would role-play. Other times we would just talk things over. But I always had Megan do some kind of practice before she left the room. At that point I would have at least some idea about how we were doing. Sometimes it was

difficult to come up with ways to practice without getting too hokey, but for me the practice was a must. I mean, it's one thing to talk about something and another to actually do it. I have to see it happen before I'm satisfied. I guess in Hands-On Training, that's called present, practice, and evaluate. In my own mind, I think of it as "the cycle."

I think there has to be more evaluation before you know you've succeeded. So I asked Megan to start dropping in and giving me short reports on how it was going. Actually I was a bit more specific than that. I asked her to try out the skills we had covered and then bring me a detailed report about how it went. I used the self-critique pattern from Hands-On Training. It worked very well. I think it did two things. It forced Megan to think things through, and it gave me the opportunity to coach and reinforce her performance. I guess you could call that my review.

Anyway, after a few months I started noticing a real change in Megan. It wasn't just that she had learned the mechanics of some management tools, but I think she was really starting to understand both herself and others better. I'll tell you one thing: today there are very few if any complaints about Megan's performance. She is very highly regarded around here.

It is clear that Jerome is a very warm human being. He really cares about other people and he will put forth a great deal of effort to help them. In many ways, Jerome sees his role of manager as that of a teacher and coach. In some ways, he is almost a father figure. But above all, Jerome is a master of the Hands-On Training method. He has practiced HOT for so long, it is almost second nature.

It happens with technical training and in management training: all too often the difference between classroom performance and job performance requires us to follow up with on-the-job training. After all, the class usually covers ideal situations, and we know the real world isn't quite that simple. To execute a job properly, use HOT to help transfer training from the classroom to the job.

# Chapter Summary

This chapter is really about three topics: opportunities to use Hands-On Training, the human side of the process, and your own decision to apply the principles in this book. People like the instructors in the accounting service company, others like Sue and Lu, and a few like Jerome really exist, putting Hands-On Training to use every day. Why not join them?

# Hands-On Training
# Instructor Guides

**6**

An instructor guide is a step-by-step "recipe" for instructors to follow when conducting training. Some instructors use different names, such as lesson plan, training plan, facilitator's guide, and so on, but they all refer to the same thing: a document that describes how to do the training. This chapter includes four instructor guides for Hands-On Training. These follow the Four-Phase Sequence described in chapter 4, but they go into a lot more detail.

Because this book may be used by instructors from many different organizations, such as factories, offices, retail stores, hospitals, and others, the instructor guides included here are generic. That is, they are written to be flexible and adaptable to your own situation. They are specific about how to do the training, but they only make suggestions about what topics to cover. For example, the equipment used in a bank may differ greatly from that used in a pharmacy or a photo lab. Yet our generic instructor guide for equipment must cover all of these situations and many more, as well. For that reason, you may want to go through each guide and adapt it to your own job. Also, some instructors like to have their instructor guides set up as a form. Many different alternatives are available, and you should feel free to choose the one you like best.

A summary of the four instructor guides follows:

- *Instructor Guide 1: Job Overview*

    If you are starting with a new trainee, this is the first instructor guide to use. Its purpose is to open the entire training process by covering "the basics," as an introduction or orientation to both the training and the job. This is where you set the tone for training by covering topics such as quality, safety, the overall work process, performance standards, and how the training will work. The job overview presents the big picture, helping the trainee to understand where he or she fits into the organization and the flow of work. This lays the groundwork for the more specific training that follows.

- *Instructor Guide 2: Equipment Familiarization*

    The first specific topic for training should be the language, nomenclature, and jargon used on the job. So we start by covering all of the hardware, software, tools, and materials that will be used or referenced by the trainee. Needless to say, this will vary greatly from one job to another, but the purpose of equipment familiarization training is always the same. It is to help the trainee learn what things look like, where they are located, and what they are called. The reason for covering the equipment before the work procedures is to build a foundation and vocabulary that will support both the instructor and trainee as they move forward. If the trainee knows this information, the trainee and instructor will be on the same wavelength as training progresses. This avoids the very confusing method of trying to cover both nomenclature and procedures at the same time.

- *Instructor Guide 3: Task Training*

    Once the trainee understands the "tools of the trade," it is time to cover how these are used to accomplish the job at hand. In this phase, each task or procedure is covered in detail, practiced by the trainee, and evaluated by the instructor. Starting with the basics, the instructor and trainee build a framework for performance. Training on each task or procedure follows the HOT POPPER technique, and training continues until the trainee masters every part of the job as required by the instructor. As the trainee practices each procedure, the instructor provides coaching for improved performance. The task training phase is where most of the learning takes place. This instructor guide is applied as a "loop." That is, you start at the beginning and follow the steps of HOT POPPER until the trainee can perform the first task, then you return to the beginning and repeat the process with the next task, and so on until all the required procedures have been covered. If you are trying to estimate the total length of your training program, you will need to make separate estimates for training on each task and then add them up.

- *Instructor Guide 4: Solo Performance*

  The final, and perhaps most critical, phase of training is covered in this instructor guide. During solo performance, the trainee is required to build upon the framework of task training by proving that he or she can do the whole job, with minimum help from the instructor. In this phase, the trainee's role is to perform the work and the instructor's role is to evaluate performance in order to determine whether or not the trainee is qualified to do the job. The length of the solo varies greatly from job to job, but it always must be long enough to provide a fair opportunity for the trainee to accomplish the training objectives and a reasonable opportunity for the instructor to make an accurate evaluation. As this phase draws to a conclusion, the instructor usually tapers off his or her involvement, and the training process blends into the work.

To use the instructor guides, we recommend that you first learn the Hands-On Training method. Then study the instructor guides and make an outline of your own specific topics for training. If you already have job documentation, a separate outline may not be needed. When you have studied these materials and prepared for training, we suggest you put the written documents away and then conduct the training. Most HOT instructors find that instructor guides are great for preparation but they get in the way during the actual training. However you choose to do it, what really counts is the effectiveness of your instruction. The instructor guides are tools to help with preparation.

# Instructor Guide 1: Job Overview

Note: The job overview is designed for new employees or those not familiar with the overall operation.

## Prepare

1. *Make up a set of samples of the following:*
   - Good quality output
   - Poor quality output
   - Quality specifications/prints
   - Quality measurement devices/gauges used

2. *Get safety equipment for each trainee.*

3. *Set up a quiet training area with chairs for each trainee and instructor. (This could be a break area.)*

4. *If you wish, make a flip chart or overhead of the main points to cover during each part of the session to help keep you on track. If you do this, you will have to make sure the equipment is available for your session. The session can cover:*
   - Job safety
   - A basic introduction to the job
   - Quality
   - Cleanliness and housekeeping
   - How the training will work

5. *Get training manuals or copies of materials that will be used by trainees as needed.*

6. *Check the work area. Make sure it is presentable.*

## Open

1. *Welcome each trainee:*
   - Explain that this session will help trainees get started but that most of the training will be done in the workplace.

- Make appropriate comments to reduce any worries the trainees have about being in a new situation. It may take a few minutes to calm them down.

2. *Introduce yourself and any other instructors.*
   - Each instructor should tell his or her
     - Name
     - Job
     - Role as a Hands-On Trainer or a presenter in this session
   - Each instructor should comment on the importance of the training and his or her personal commitment to helping trainees learn their jobs.

3. *Ask the trainees to introduce themselves. Have each one tell*
   - His or her name
   - Something about his or her work background
   - How he or she feels about this job.

4. *Introduce the topics that will be covered in this session:*
   - Safety
   - An overview of the work process
   - Quality
   - Cleanliness and housekeeping
   - How the training will work

5. *Ask if there are any initial questions, and answer as needed.*

## Present: Safety

Note: Jobs vary greatly when it comes to safety. Cover only those safety topics that apply to your particular situation.

1. *Explain that there are several really important safety factors on this job.*

2. *Cover the following as they apply to the job:*
   - Noise
   - Eye safety
   - Personal protective equipment (hand out as needed)
   - Moving parts and pinch points

- Knives, blades, or other sharp objects
- Electrical shock
- Lock out/tag out procedures
- Fumes and dust
- Hazardous materials
- Floor hazards and falls
- Safety around vehicles
- Safe driving practices
- Lifting procedures
- Fire hazards
- Explosive hazards
- Climbing and falls
- First aid
- Emergency procedures
- Other topics based upon your experience

## Present: Work Process Overview

Note: The point in this session is just to familiarize trainees with the work process and the area, not to give the details.

*1. Take trainees to the work area.*

*2. Briefly show and explain how the work is done:*
- Stick to the main steps only.
- Answer questions as you go. You will need to defer many of the answers till later in the training. Don't be afraid to explain that you'll cover something later.
- Review safety and point out areas of specific hazards.

*3. When the tour is complete, take the trainees back to the training area.*

## Present: Quality

*1. Explain the importance of quality:*
- Explain the organization's quality policy and/or philosophy (sometimes it is best to have specialists do this part).

- Explain the trainees' personal responsibilities for quality.
- Hold a question-and-answer session.

2. *Distribute and briefly explain the set of product samples:*
- Show examples of both good products and defects.
- Let trainees handle the samples for a few minutes, then collect the samples.
- Hold a brief question-and-answer session.
- Show and explain samples of product specifications/prints, and explain where these are located.
- Show and explain any special measurement devices (instruments, rulers, tapes, gauges, etc.).
- If there is time, have trainees use them.
- Tell trainees that you will explain more about quality and how to maintain it as the trainees learn the job.

3. *Demonstrate how to*
- Inspect the work outputs
- Fill out quality forms

# Present: Cleanliness and Housekeeping

1. *Explain the importance of good housekeeping:*
- It helps prevent accidents.
- It helps maintain quality.
- It is important for the organization's public image.

2. *Briefly cover the expectations for cleanliness and housekeeping.*

3. *Explain that you will cover a lot more on housekeeping as they learn the job. For now, list the various housekeeping issues that will be covered later in the training.*

4. *Ask and answer questions as needed.*

# Present: The Training Process

1. *Explain how the training will work. Explain that you will cover the following subjects:*
- Equipment familiarization

- Basic work procedures
- Practice doing the job

2. *Explain that most of the training sessions will use the following pattern:*
   - Opening to introduce the subject
   - Presentation of information about the subject
   - Practice of skills and procedures
   - Evaluation and coaching from the instructor
   - Review of the session

3. *Explain that most of the training will be Hands-On Training done in the work area.*

4. *Tell the trainees that you expect them to ask lots of questions and get really involved in the training. Explain that it is better to ask questions and make mistakes now than once they're on the job.*

5. *Explain the objective/goal of training.*

6. *Explain how trainees will be evaluated at the end of training.*

7. *Ask if they have any questions about how the training will work, and answer as needed.*

8. *Hand out and explain any training materials to be used.*
   - Explain how they are to be used.
   - Cover the policy on returning them after training.

## Review

1. *Briefly review the topics covered during this session:*
   - Safety
   - Work process
   - Quality
   - Cleanliness and housekeeping
   - The training process

2. *Answer any final questions.*

3. *Move on to the next session.*

# Instructor Guide 2: Equipment Familiarization

Note: The point of this session is to acquaint the trainees with the names, locations, and features of the main equipment used on the job. That way when you begin teaching the work procedures, you can expect they will understand the language of the job.

## Prepare

*1. Make sure the work area is presentable.*

*2. If you have equipment documentation, use it.*

*3. If you don't have equipment documentation, make a list of items to cover. Include items such as*

- Hardware and main features
- Software systems
- Documentation
- Office equipment
- Machines, main features, and controls
- Tools
- Instruments
- Gauges
- Fixtures
- Fasteners
- Raw materials and supplies
- Chemicals
- Parts and subassemblies
- Vehicles, main features, and controls
- Construction equipment
- Protective clothing and equipment
- Storage areas and devices
- Housekeeping equipment and supplies
- Transportation systems
- Control systems
- Maintenance equipment
- Security systems
- Emergency equipment

- Utilities
- Information processing systems

*4. If you wish, set up a display of tools and/or equipment used on the job.*

## Open

*1. Explain that this session is about the equipment*

- Systems
- Main features
- Controls
- Tools of the trade

*2. Tell the trainees that it is important to remember the parts and what they are called because you will be referring to them all the time during training.*

*3. Assure them that for now, they don't have to worry about the work. Instead, they should just focus on where items are located, what they are called, and generally how they work.*

## Present, Practice, and Evaluate: Equipment Parts and Purposes

Note: Equipment familiarization should be covered with all basic trainees and for those advanced workers moving into new areas.

*1. Follow the equipment documentation or your own list of topics to cover:*

- Be sure to use the correct names.
- If parts are sometimes called other names, explain what you want trainees to call them.
- Stick to how systems work.
- Avoid getting into the work procedures used. This will take too much time and confuse trainees.
- Give only enough detail to help trainees understand, and avoid information they don't really need.
- Remember: Too much information can be very confusing.

2. *During your explanation, ask and answer questions to make sure trainees understand.*

3. *Be sure to explain anything special like safety precautions or special maintenance needs.*

4. *When you are finished, have trainees practice explaining the equipment:*
   - Point out some of the main parts.
   - Have trainees name them and explain them.
   - Provide help and additional information as needed.

## Review

1. *Go over the main points from the session.*

2. *Ask and answer any final questions.*

3. *When you are ready, move on to the next session.*

# Instructor Guide 3: Task Training

Note: Repeat the following pattern for each task learned by the trainees.

## Prepare

1. *Use existing job documentation or make a list of all tasks, methods, skills, and work procedures the trainees will need to know.*

2. *Decide on the best sequence for training:*
   - Sometimes there is an immediate need for job performance on certain tasks. Start with these.
   - In some cases, basic tasks should be mastered before moving on to more advanced tasks. Start with the basics.
   - In other cases, the advanced tasks may help trainees learn the basics, as well. If so, cover the more advanced tasks first.
   - Whenever possible, start with those tasks that make it easier to learn others that follow.

3. *Before starting task training, review the task(s) you will cover.*

4. *Assemble all tools, equipment, and materials needed to perform each task.*

5. *Make sure the work area is set up the way you want it to be. Be sure it is neat, clean, and orderly: the way you expect it to look every day.*

6. *As the instructor, you must decide how much time to spend on each task.*

## Open

1. *State the task.*

2. *Explain the importance of doing it right.*

3. *Mention any special safety or quality points that apply to the task.*

## Present: Procedures

1. *Follow all of the correct procedures, showing and explaining how to perform the task. Follow this training method:*
   - Position trainees where they can see and hear.
   - Go slowly step-by-step.
   - Be very systematic.
   - Point out any "tricks of the trade" that will make the trainees' job easier.
   - Hold a question-and-answer session to make sure trainees understand.

2. *Repeat the demonstration at least twice, moving a little faster each time.*
   - Have the trainees explain the task as you do the work.
   - Make corrections as needed.

3. *When you are ready, move on.*

## Practice and Evaluate: Procedures

1. *Follow this general pattern:*

2. *Explain the importance of doing the job right first and then building up speed.*
   - Have trainees perform the task while you watch and evaluate.
   - Observe carefully and provide coaching as needed.
   - Be sure to stand where you can see trainees' work.
   - Ask questions to make sure trainees understand what they're doing.
   - Have them repeat steps as needed.
   - Give them tips on how to improve. Do this just before you have them repeat the task.
   - Have them repeat the whole demonstration at least twice.
   - The second time through, ask trainees to explain what they're doing as they go.
   - Stand back a little.

- Evaluate performance.
- Continue practice till you are satisfied that trainees can do the job. Then move on.

*3. Repeat this training method for each procedure.*

## Review

*1. Briefly review the main points from the session, stressing safety and quality.*

*2. Ask and answer any final questions.*

*3. Release trainees, assign work, or move on to the next task as appropriate.*

# Instructor Guide 4: Solo Performance

Note: This section of the training should start after the trainees have completed practice on each specific task. The operating practice section is intended to allow trainees to practice the whole job under guidance from the instructor. As the instructor gains more confidence in the trainees' ability, he or she should begin to taper off guidance till the trainees are essentially on their own.

## Prepare

1. *For this session, get everything ready for operations on the job.*

2. *Decide on the length of time for practice:*
   - It should be long enough to be sure the trainees can actually do the job.
   - In some cases, this session may last up to several weeks.

## Open

1. *Explain that this part of training will be spent practicing the whole job.*

2. *Explain how long the practice will last.*

3. *Explain that the trainees' assignment is to do the job and the instructor's job is to observe performance, offer suggestions for improvement, and help in any way possible.*

4. *Explain to the trainees that you will be available if they need help:*
   - Explain that if they have any questions or if they get stuck, they should contact you.
   - Be sure to state where you will be.
   - Emphasize that they should try to find you before getting help from anybody else.

5. *Explain that if they can't find you, they should put aside any questionable work outputs or production and hold them till you return. Meanwhile, they should continue to work.*

6. *Answer any questions.*

7. *Move on.*

## Practice and Evaluate: Job Performance

1. *Make job assignments to trainees.*

2. *Have them begin work.*

3. *During the practice session, check trainees frequently:*
   - Make sure they're following the procedures you taught them.
   - If they need help, provide it.
   - Ask lots of questions to make sure trainees really understand what they're doing.

4. *If and when trainees get into trouble, help them out.*
   - It is your job to handle anything that happens beyond the basics assigned to new operators.
   - If you need to perform complex tasks with the controls, it is recommended that you *don't* try to teach these to new trainees. They aren't ready.
   - Use problems and critical incidents to discuss an operator's proper response to these events.

5. *Be sure to double-check trainees' work outputs to make sure they're acceptable.*

6. *About twice per day, have the trainees critique their own performance:*
   - What went right?
   - What went wrong?
   - What did they learn?

7. *As time goes on, taper off your contact with the trainees. Remember: The point is to get trainees ready to operate their own.*

## Review the Training Program

1. *Remind trainees about the subjects covered in the training.*

2. *Give trainees your impressions about how they did in training. If completion of training results in job qualification, inform the trainees of results.*

3. *Ask if they have any final questions.*

4. *Thank the trainees for their participation.*

5. *Release the trainees.*

# Making Hands-On Training Work

It is one matter to start using Hands-On Training in place of traditional on-the-job training and another to keep it going. Unfortunate though it may be, the U.S. business community has a long history of embracing and quickly discarding new programs. A "been there, done that" mentality is firmly implanted in the minds of both managers and workers. This being the case, it is no wonder that many, perhaps even most, new programs are greeted with passive resistance from those who remain convinced that if they can just wait it out, "This, too, shall pass!" Hands-On Training is no exception.

To help you overcome this resistance, we looked at organizations that are committed to making Hands-On Training work to find out what characteristics they share. Most of these fall into the "lessons learned" category. As with just about everything having to do with HOT, the following suggestions, derived from these lessons, are simple and straightforward.

# Let the Workers Make It Work

This is probably the single most important piece of advice we can offer about using Hands-On Training on a long-term basis. Most of the other suggestions are intended to support the notion that HOT should belong to the workers themselves. It should not be regarded as a "management program." In fact, HOT shouldn't be regarded as a program at all. Rather, HOT should become an integral part of "the way we do things here."

Hands-On Training works best when it is virtually invisible. For example, new employees are assigned to an instructor as a matter of course. There is no question about it. When a worker needs to learn a new skill, he or she connects with an instructor and together they set up the required training. There is no need for complex administrative procedures because the people sustain their own training efforts. If records of training are required, the workers should maintain them. It sounds so simple to make training a normal part of work, but there are a couple of factors that can make or break the effort. These include management support, accessibility of the training, and the way the training system is structured.

# Get Management Support

In this case, we have two very specific suggestions about how management can support Hands-On Training. First, if HOT is the workers' system, managers need to let them use it. The most commonly expressed fear of managers is that "people will turn this workplace into a training center." Not so. Today's workers are almost painfully aware of the need to remain competitive. They are not about to waste time doing unnecessary training. On the other hand, HOT instructors tend to take their responsibilities very seriously. They usually insist on spending enough time to do the training correctly. They become concerned when managers demand unrealistic shortcuts.

No matter how badly managers need instantaneous job performance, they must accept the facts: Training isn't particularly efficient and job performance doesn't occur by magic. It takes time to conduct effective training. The most commonly heard complaint of HOT instructors is that managers demand the impossible.

Hands-On Training is definitely a "pay me now or pay me later" situation. The cost of doing it properly in the first place may be obvious, but this is far outweighed by the even higher (but hidden) cost of workers who are poorly trained due to unrealistic time limits.

The second element of management support is the clarification of responsibilities for training throughout the organization—not just for instructors. Most organizations have a chain of leadership. Each level may include different responsibilities for training. We suggest that these be defined as part of the organization's effort to establish accountability. For example, a top level executive may be responsible for establishing philosophy and policy. A local manager may be responsible for defining how the policy will be implemented in his or her business unit. A supervisor or team leader may be responsible to provide support (time, equipment, assistance, etc.) for the training effort. The instructor is responsible for delivering the training as planned, and the trainee is responsible for receiving the training. All of these responsibilities are related, yet each reflects an individual's unique role in the process. In this way, the people who carry out the effort will be more likely to make the training work as planned.

# Make Training Accessible

One of the most common of all problems associated with job training in the United States is that the training is difficult to get. Workers who need to learn new skills are forced to wait for a class to begin or for the only instructor to become available. Time is wasted, and frustration with the whole process tends to grow.

Hands-On Training should be readily accessible when it is needed. Again, this statement has a couple of major implications. First, an organization must have an adequate number of trained instructors to satisfy the demand for training. It is usually a mistake to make only one or two people responsible for all instruction. When this is done, the rationale is usually that "these instructors are the best qualified people we have." What difference does that make when the trainees can't get the training they need? We would suggest that it is better to have more instructors, even if you must accept a degree of trade-off between availability and skill.

To maintain a cadre of instructors, the organization needs to provide instructor training on a regular basis due to turnover. Job changes, transfers, and changes in one's personal situation may all cause instructor turnover, and to keep the training effort going, those who leave the job must be replaced. We are *not* suggesting that being an instructor is a full-time job. Rather, in most organizations it is a part-time responsibility that is easily overlooked when thinking about staffing. But the more the cadre of instructors shrinks due to turnover, the more difficult it will be for people to get Hands-On Training. This, in turn, will reduce the effectiveness of the training effort. Periodic instructor training will automatically replenish the pool of HOT instructors and maintain the availability of training.

## Maintain Job Documentation

Job documentation ranges all the way from simple outlines made by instructors to elaborate systems that are developed by professionals. It doesn't matter. The documentation, whatever it is, must be maintained or Hands-On Training can grind to a halt. To maintain training documentation, the organization must find ways to gather the information for required updates. Then it must provide periodic maintenance that includes an approval process and a means to build changes into the documentation.

Some companies are tempted to keep no training documentation at all. That way there is no need for maintenance. The problem with this approach is that training without documentation may lead to a return to traditional unstructured on-the-job training, where serious problems with consistency occur. Documentation merely provides one more degree of assurance that the training is repeatable, an essential ingredient in HOT. While the HOT POPPER method can work without documentation, it is more effective and certainly more consistent when standard job procedures are defined.

# Keep It Simple

Training has a way of becoming complicated. Sometimes it is complicated by its own delivery system. Sometimes training is complicated by bureaucracy and sometimes by micromanagement. These are all problems to avoid when using Hands-On Training.

When training professionals manage programs, a degree of complexity is acceptable because these people are educated to deal with elaborate training systems. However, this is definitely not the case with most HOT instructors. Usually instructors are experts in doing their jobs and trained to use the techniques of Hands-On Training as an adjunct to their regular work. They are not comfortable dealing with complicated training, documentation, and administrative systems. In fact, it is probably safe to say that the more complex the training system, the less likely HOT instructors are to use it.

If we are truly interested in integrating training as a normal part of work, we must take care to avoid making the system look like a program. In fact, job training is not a program. Properly applied, it is an ongoing support system more akin to equipment maintenance or quality assurance than any passing fad. Hands-On Training just happens to be a very effective method for accomplishing a function that must be accomplished anyway. A simple job training system, supported by a simple method and simple rules, stands a far better chance of success in the workplace than a complex training system that requires heavy maintenance and administration.

# The Training Professional's Role in Hands-On Training

Hands-On Training differs from other types of training in some important ways, which have been described in this book. However, HOT also shares the key ingredients that make any kind of training effective: it is targeted and it is systematic. Professional trainers can add an important dimension to the HOT effort, especially by providing support for the instructors who are charged with delivering the training to those who need it. Here are a few suggestions as to how training professionals can augment an organization's efforts:

- Establish the system.
- Help define responsibilities and accountability.
- Train and coach HOT instructors.
- Assist with training documentation.
- Develop simple administrative procedures.
- Act as custodian for materials.
- Hold periodic instructor meetings.
- Represent HOT instructors to management.
- Evaluate the training effort and recommend improvements.

Many organizations apply Hands-On Training without a training professional. But in organizations that have a professional trainer on staff, two different approaches seem to be used. One is that the training professional *controls* the training. The other is that he or she stays in the background and *supports* the training effort. Of these, the second approach is more successful because it keeps the responsibility for job training where it belongs: with those who do the work.

# Chapter Summary

Hands-On Training works best when it is integrated as a part of everyday work. It is better if the workers manage their own system than if HOT is a "management program." The training must be accessible, documentation must be maintained, and the system must be simple. Training professionals can add an important dimension by providing support systems for the HOT effort.

# Conclusion
## Harnessing Human Nature

Hands-On Training represents a departure from traditional on-the-job training, merely by the addition of structure. While this may not be an entirely new concept, it is certainly one that is all too frequently overlooked in the workplace. As proven by both research and experience, the simple act of structuring on-the-job training greatly increases its efficiency and effectiveness. And best of all, it's not complicated! Hands-On Training is the ideal informal training method. It may be implemented at any level in any organization where an experienced worker needs to show an inexperienced worker how to do a job.

In a very real sense, Hands-On Training is nothing more than an orderly approach to something that is going to happen anyway. With or without the structure of HOT POPPER, inexperienced workers will try to learn their jobs from experienced workers—it's human nature. Hands-On Training harnesses this aspect of human nature in order to speed up the learning process. As a HOT instructor, this is part and parcel of your job.

Hands-On Training has changed the lives of many people, both instructors and trainees. A few of their stories are included in this book. For most trainees, Hands-On Training simply makes their lives easier because it makes their jobs easier. For HOT instructors, however, the rewards may be great. I have trained thousands of instructors, and I have seen many of them achieve more personal growth than they ever thought possible. One such person was a young man from Georgia whose reading and writing skills were far below average. At the same time, this young man was very good at his job and eager to teach others his skills. He was trained as a HOT instructor, and he gained so much respect from fellow employees that he was promoted to a team leadership position. He went back to school and graduated. Today he is the manager of a major department for his company. Hands-On Training was his springboard to a successful career, and I hope it will be yours too.

# Notes

1. R. A. Swanson and S. A. Sawzin, *Industrial Training Research Project* (Bowling Green, Ohio: Bowling Green State University, 1975).

2. C. R. Dooley, *The Training within Industry Report, 1910–1945* (Washington, D.C.: War Manpower Commission Bureau of Training, Training within Industry Service, 1945).

3. R. A. Swanson and S. A. Sawzin, *Industrial Training Research Project* (Bowling Green, Ohio: Bowling Green State University, 1975).

# Selected References

Cullen, G., G. Sisson, S. Sawzin, and R. A. Swanson. "Training, What's It Worth? An Experimental Case Study at Johns Manville." *Training and Development Journal* 30, no. 9 (1976): 12–20.

This journal article reports on data from a study that compares structured on-the-job training to unstructured on-the-job (trial-and-error) training of new workers who were put on the job under the supervision of busy supervisors. Compared to those receiving unstructured on-the-job training, the structured on-the-job trainees reached competence in about 30 percent of the time, had a 130 percent increase in solved production problems, and had large savings related to maintaining production rates and utilizing raw materials.

Davis, J. R., and A. B. Davis. *Effective Training Strategies: A Comprehensive Guide to Maximizing Learning in Organizations.* San Francisco: Berrett-Koehler, 1998.

This book formally recognizes that adults in the workplace need to develop a variety of skills, which demands a variety of learning strategies and activities. Davis and Davis identify seven strategies for seven categories of workplace skills to be learned. The strategies include behavioral, cognitive, inquiry, mental, virtual, holistic, and group dynamics. Specific implementation techniques for each strategy are covered.

Dooley, C. R. *The Training within Industry Report, 1910–1945.* Washington, D.C.: War Manpower Commission Bureau of Training, Training within Industry Service, 1945.

The Training within Industry (TWI) effort during World War II is seen as a watershed event for the training profession and the origin of the contemporary human resource development profession. One of the most notable aspects of TWI was the massive utilization of the famous four-step training method, the forerunner of Hands-on Training. Dooley reports in detail on the utilization of this method of on-the-job training and the training of subject-matter experts in becoming trainers.

Jacobs, R. L., and M. J. Jones. *Structured On-the-Job Training: Unleashing Employee Expertise in the Workplace.* San Francisco: Berrett-Koehler, 1995.

This book discusses the system and strategy required for professional trainers to manage structured on-the-job training as a major way for organizations to meet their training needs. The core method in this book is to keep a systematic on-the-job training effort in the hands of training professionals who are assisted by subject-matter experts. The Jacobs and Jones book is complementary to this book, *Hands-On Training,* which is meant to be put directly into the hands of subject-matter experts—supervisors and expert workers—who are responsible for training activity.

Swanson, R. A., and S. A. Sawzin. *Industrial Training Research Project.* Bowling Green, Ohio: Bowling Green State University, 1975.

The purpose of this study was to conduct an experimental comparison of the structured versus unstructured training of semiskilled workers. This classic study made several contributions to the training profession. This report originated the term "structured on-the-job training." Prior to this, the literature talked about on-the-job training and classroom training with the implicit understanding that on-the-job training was unstructured and classroom training was structured. This study opened up the people's thinking to recognize the existence of structured and unstructured classroom training and structured and unstructured on-the-job training. Training structure, not location, became the essential variable.

# Index

## A

accessibility of training, 91–92
acronyms
    *coach,* 51–53
    HOT POPPER, 13, 37–38
analysis of jobs, 17
anxiety felt by instructor, 18
applying Hands-On Training (examples)
    evolution, 59–62
    execution, 66–69
    revolution, 62–65
    training instructors, 39–46
assembling training materials, 19
assignments, 33, 52

## B

barriers to good performance, 30
Bowling Green Study, 9
buddy system, 9

## C

certification, 55
chain loss, 5
changes, learning incremental, 8
characteristics of Hands-On Training, 16–17, 36–37
cleanliness, 78
*coach* acronym, 51–53
coaches. *See* instructors

## D

coaching
    elements of, 51–53
    essence of, 44
    helpful/unhelpful, 30–31
comfort zones of instructors, 45–46
communicating ideas for improvement, 52
complimenting trainees, 52
consistency, 24
creating dependency on instructor, 34
criticism, avoiding/eliminating, 30

## D

daily routine, 53–54
dangerous steps, practicing, 27
demonstrating the job, 22–26, 48–49, 78. *See also* presenting the subject
dependency, creating, 34
development of Hands-On Training, 13
difficult parts of job, 31
dilution of a skill, 5
displaying tools/equipment, 81
distortion of a skill, 5
distractions, 49
documentation of jobs
    maintaining, 92
    official method, 24
    for training programs, 17
    when not to use, 19

# About the Author

Gary R. Sisson has been active in the training and development profession since 1966. Prior to founding Paradigm Corporation in 1982, he was in charge of all management and technical training for Johns Manville Corporation, a Fortune 500 firm with 36,000 employees. Since founding Paradigm's international consulting practice, Gary has worked toward perfecting Hands-On Training (HOT) as a means of adding structure and effectiveness to traditional forms of on-the-job training. Paradigm advises clients on HOT, develops HOT systems, and trains instructors to use the skills explained in this book.

Gary's clients have included companies such as CertainTeed Corporation, Insteel Wire Products, TRW Safety Systems, Keystone Foods, Diesel Technology, The DeVilbiss Company, Northwest Airlines, Hendrickson Suspension Systems, Synergen (now part of Amgen), Amoco Production Company, Cadillac Plastics, Wilson Trailer Company, SPX, Fortress Scientific, Mastic Corporation, Somatogen, Johns Manville, and many others. He has served as a guest lecturer at Bowling Green State University, the University of Northern Iowa, and the University of Minnesota and has published articles in most of the human resource development journals. In addition, Gary has served as the training advisor to a commission of the Colorado state government.

To learn more about Gary Sisson and the services offered by Paradigm Corporation, call (303) 797-2415 or visit the Web site www.handsontraining.org.

# Berrett-Koehler Publishers

ERRETT-KOEHLER is an independent publisher of books, periodicals, and other publications at the leading edge of new thinking and innovative practice on work, business, management, leadership, stewardship, career development, human resources, entrepreneurship, and global sustainability.

Since the company's founding in 1992, we have been committed to supporting the movement toward a more enlightened world of work by publishing books, periodicals, and other publications that help us to integrate our values with our work and work lives, and to create more humane and effective organizations.

We have chosen to focus on the areas of work, business, and organizations, because these are central elements in many people's lives today. Furthermore, the work world is going through tumultuous changes, from the decline of job security to the rise of new structures for organizing people and work. We believe that change is needed at all levels—individual, organizational, community, and global—and our publications address each of these levels.

We seek to create new lenses for understanding organizations, to legitimize topics that people care deeply about but that current business orthodoxy censors or considers secondary to bottom-line concerns, and to uncover new meaning, means, and ends for our work and work lives.

See next pages for other books from Berrett-Koehler Publishers

# Structured On-the-Job Training

## Unleashing Employee Expertise in the Workplace

Ronald Jacobs and Michael Jones

Jacobs and Jones describe an approach to on-the-job training that combines the structure of off-site training with the inherent efficiency of training conducted in the actual job setting. They show how structured OJT helps employees bridge the gap between learning job information and actually using that information on the job.

Hardcover, 220 pages • ISBN 1-881052-20-6 CIP
Item #52206-371 $29.95

# Training Across Multiple Locations

## Developing a System that Works

Stephen Krempl and R. Wayne Pace

*Training Across Multiple Locations* is about how to design, build, and assess an effective training organization that is spread across multiple locations. It provides a model to guide in the development of the system, a questionnaire to review the various locations, and several suggestions to ensure plans can be executed within the organization. It shows how distance learning technology, including intranets, web-based training, and computer-based training are central to managing multi-point training.

Hardcover, 250 pages • ISBN 1-57675-157-0 CIP
Item #51570-371 $34.95

# Love 'Em or Lose 'Em

## Getting Good People to Stay

Beverly Kaye and Sharon Jordan-Evans

It happens time and time again: the brightest and most talented people leave the company for "better opportunities." Their peers wonder how management could let them go. Their managers feel helpless to make them stay. Beverly Kaye and Sharon Jordan-Evans explore the truth behind the dissatisfactions of many of today's workers and offer 26 strategies—from A to Z—that managers can use to address their concerns and keep them on the team.

Paperback original, 244 pages • ISBN 1-57675-073-6 CIP
Item #50736-371 $17.95

**Berrett-Koehler Publishers**
PO Box 565, Williston, VT 05495-9900
Call toll-free! **800-929-2929** 7 am-12 midnight
Or fax your order to 802-864-7627
For fastest service order online: **www.bkconnection.com**

# Performance Consulting

Moving Beyond Training

Dana Gaines Robinson and James C. Robinson

*Performance Consulting* provides a conceptual framework and many how-to's for moving from the role of a traditional trainer to that of a performance consultant. Useful tools, illustrative exercises, and a case study show how the techniques described are applied.

Paperback, 320 pages • ISBN 1-881052-84-2 CIP
Item #52842-371  $24.95

Hardcover • ISBN 1-881052-30-3 CIP • Item #52303-371  $34.95

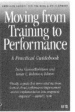

# Moving from Training to Performance

A Practical Guidebook

Dana Gaines Robinson and
James C. Robinson, Editors

*Moving from Training to Performance* shows how today's performance improvement departments can take a more active role in helping organizations meet their goals. It offers practical, action-oriented techniques from some of the most highly respected contributors in the field—Geoff Bellman, Geary Rummler, Paul Elliott, Erica Keeps, and others—paired with real-life case studies of organizations that have achieved exceptional results by successfully making the transition to performance at each level of alignment.

Paperback, 300 pages • ISBN 1-57675-039-6 CIP
Item #50396-371  $29.95

# Human Resource Development Research Handbook

Linking Research and Practice

Richard A. Swanson and Elwood F. Holton III, Editors

*Human Resource Development Research Handbook* gives practitioners the tools they need to stay on the leading edge of the profession. Each chapter is written in straightforward language by a leading researcher and offers real-world examples to show how research and theory are not just for academics, but are practical tools to solve everyday problems.

Paperback, 225 pages • ISBN 1-881052-68-0 CIP
Item #52680-371  $24.95

**Berrett-Koehler Publishers**
PO Box 565, Williston, VT 05495-9900
Call toll-free! **800-929-2929** 7 am-12 midnight
Or fax your order to 802-864-7627
For fastest service order online: **www.bkconnection.com**

BK